MY NAME IS

JACKSON

Letters from a rescue dog

By

Diarmuid E Fahy

Illustrated by

Kathy Tiernan

My Name is Jackson

978-1-3999-7149-2

Illustrations by Kathy Tiernan – www.fairlyart.com

To Dad

Who would have loved Jackson, and Jackson would have loved him back.

For Julia.

Preface

The first dog I can remember was a solid liver German Shorthaired Pointer named Pollock. He was my Dad's dog, and he was beautiful. Pollock's primary role was to be a hunting dog (and he was very good at his job) but he was an integral part of our family. He was gentle and loving and loyal, and absolutely adored my Dad. He was fond of the rest of us - particularly my granny - but Dad was his entire world. For me, he was always the epitome of what a Good Dog should be, so when the time finally arrived that I as an adult could consider having a dog of my own, there was never a question but it would be a GSP.

The wrinkle, however, was that we wanted to be responsible people and give home to a rescue dog. We knew it would be practically impossible to find a GSP in a UK rescue, so we set our search for overseas. One group in particular stood out for us. They specifically rehomed pointers from Cyprus to the UK, had a large active community over here, but above all seemed to care so very deeply about the dogs they helped.

So it came to pass that in January 2021, we filled out our application form for Apollo's Angels/Rehoming Cyprus Pointers, adding maps, pictures and satellite photographs of where we lived, desperately hoping we'd pass muster and be able to join the queue for one of their dogs. "Fritz looks like a nice boy", I

i

added to my closing comments, referring to a skinny dog with a big head whose photo had just been uploaded to Facebook that day. And we waited.

I had expected that it would be weeks, if not months before we heard anything, but a few days later the phone rang, and a 90-minute conversation ensued. It was very gently done, but was definitely an interrogation, and a reality check about the work needed to rehabilitate these dogs. Rose-tinted glasses well and truly discarded, this was followed by a second long conversation a couple of days later, at the end of which we were asked if we'd like to offer Fritz a home. I can remember feeling my heart hammering in my chest, as I tried to remain calm and say "yes" without coming across as a gibbering idiot and completely destroying this huge opportunity.

And that was it. Well almost. As this was in the time of Covid, onsite home checking wasn't possible, so the final step was to do a video walkthrough of the house and gardens, pointing out walls and fences and access points. I also pointed out where he would sleep and eat and where he'd play and where we'd sit for cuddles, and how nicely a dog would fit into our home and our lives. I'm not sure everyone else did a 15-minute mini-movie, but I wasn't taking any chances.

The second complication was that at the time he was rescued, he was a little bag of bones, and was going to have to spend at least another month in rehabilitation before he would be fit enough to make the trip from Cyprus. Again because of the Pandemic, the journey was made even more arduous because there were no practical direct flights to the UK and he was going to have to do a whistle-stop tour of northern Europe before finally making it to us.

And so it came to pass that approaching midnight on the night of March 21st 2021 found us sitting impatiently in the car park of a motorway services on the M25, waiting for a transport van that we thought would never arrive. But it did. And in the biggest crate in the back of the van was the most beautiful dog I had ever seen in my life. The handler put my slip around his neck, lifted him down, and handed me the lead.

I bent down, stroked Jackson's head and said "Bravo, big lad". Even though he was tired and scared he looked up at me, gave a single wag of his tail, and that was it. My life - our lives - were intertwined and irreversibly changed forever.

Diarmuid Fahy, October 2023.

iv

A long journey – Everything changes – A new friend

25th March 2021

Master Milo Sellick, Zummerzet

Dear Milo

Thank you very much for such a great present! Hare is wonderful and I've put her very carefully in my bed with HedgePig and my pheasant Phezzie. It's very kind of you to be so generous to a visitor from a faraway place. I've never met a Labradoodle before, but I'm a German Shorthaired Pointer and they tell me I'm a big lad. If I was a very posh dog, they'd say I was Liver and White Patched and Flecked but I'm not posh so I'm just brown and white. I've seen the growing three times now so I'm a grown up dog. I live somewhere a long, long way away that's very different from here. It's hot and dry and there wasn't always a lot to eat and you got tied up for a long time. Sometimes you got to help The Man look for birds. I really liked that but got shouted at when I got things wrong. Sometimes it was worse, when The Man got really angry.

That all changed a little while ago when I went to live with a Lovely Lady who had lots and lots of other dogs. There was plenty to eat and I got to play a LOT! The lady called me Fritz, but I had a different name before that and I think I had another one before that too but I don't remember as it was a long time ago.

A few days ago, then, everything changed again. The Lovely Lady brought me and a lot of my friends to a big place in the middle of the night where I was put into a really big box and after a long time got into a huge big car that goes up in the air. There were loads of us - me and my friends and more dogs than I could count. I don't know if you've been up in the air but I don't recommend it. It's noisy and bumpy and makes your tummy feel funny. I didn't like it and was quite scared. After ages there was a big bump and then after being poked and examined again I got into another big car with lots of other dogs and we were off driving again.

After the longest time (would you believe it was actually night-time again!) we stopped and a lady took my friend Indra away. Then she opened my door, put a new lead around my neck and lifted me out to the ground. It was a strange dark place and there were lots of people around and I was very scared. I then heard someone gently say "Bravo, big lad" just like the lady I lived with. I looked up and there was a tall man standing next to me who seemed very happy. He reached down and put a new collar with another lead around my neck and then he stroked my head. That was nice so I gave my tail a little wag. He seemed to want me to go with him and I was a bit unsure, but he reminded me of the Lovely Lady so I went along. We then got to another car where another really nice lady was waiting. I liked her straight away, and not just because of the yummy food she had for me. After eating a big bowl of chicken and rice I climbed into the back of the car and settled down for the journey to wherever we were going. I hoped it was home as I was really, really tired. The man got into the seat beside me so I put my head and paws on his lap. It just seemed the right thing to do. This made him blow his nose and wipe his eyes for some reason. He kept stroking me and telling me I was a Good Boy and who was I to disagree.

In the end we came to another place where after more food and a wander outside while the man held my lead it was time for bed. This place is a bit strange, I thought. There was obviously another dog here because there were loads and loads of dog things - a lovely bed, toys, blankets - but it didn't smell of dog at all. In any case, I hoped they didn't mind me borrowing their things but I was so sleepy I just got into the bed, closed my eyes and drifted off, thinking I might go back tomorrow.

I'm feeling sleepy again now, so I'll say goodnight and tell you more in my next letter. Thank you again for Hare. I'll take really good care of her.

Your friend,

Fritz

26th March 2021

Dear Milo

I hope you're well and happy and having a nice day.

I've been having a really interesting time here and am enjoying my visit very much. The people I'm staying with are very nice and kind. There is LOTS of food to eat, and I'm getting used to not having to share it, but I forget every now and then and get a bit scared if something moves behind me while I'm having my dinner. I think the foreign food, even though I love it, doesn't love me and I've had a dodgy tummy for a couple of days but I'm feeling much better now. I've been having cheese, which is wonderful. Do you like cheese?

It's quite chilly here though, but I've been loaned a coat and some pyjamas so am managing to stay nice and toasty. It's a lot of fun putting them on and the man always looks cross to start with and then starts laughing when I try to help but when he uses his boss voice I stand still and let him do up the buckles. The lady has a boss voice too, but she laughs more. I really like her. She's only little so very close to me and that's nice.

This place is very quiet and we don't see many cars at all. We go out a lot, and the Boss Man fusses about with a strappy thing that clicks onto me and a different collar with a box on it before we go outside. I think it all looks very smart and I get excited when he takes it off the hook by the door and wiggle my bum a lot. Sometimes the Boss Man and I go out to walk on our own and sometimes the Boss Lady comes with us. I love going outside! There are so many things to smell and see and always something exciting happening. The people talk to me when I get too excited though, and give me a cuddle if I get scared of something I've never seen before. Today we saw a cloud of smoke come out of a hole in the side of the house and that was not nice, but the Boss Man took me near it and it wasn't smoke at all but like warm water. It was actually very nice!

We go outside before breakfast, before lunch and again before it gets dark. We meet people all the time and they are always happy to meet me. Everyone we see wants to give me a cuddle and that's fine by me, although it seems they never get close to other people these days. They all say I'm very handsome and a good boy. Yesterday though we met some other dogs! They are all Golden Retrievers and live nearby, all in the same house. The people stopped to talk so I got to know the dogs at the same time. Welly is very old so he doesn't play very much. Bonnie is younger and is very nice. She is a hunting dog like I was but I think she doesn't make as many mistakes as me. And then there was Scrumpy. Scrumpy is a big puppy and VERY bouncy! They made me very welcome and said this is a great place to live. They're very lucky to be able to stay here all the time. I miss the Lovely Lady and my friends but I'll be very sad to leave here when my holiday ends.

There are lots and lots of birds around here and sometimes I lose myself so much in that amazing smell. You know what it's like: the smell comes in your nose and fills your head so much there's no room for anything else and all that matters is searching and searching until you find where it's come from and then you creep up veeery slowly so the bird doesn't see you and then you stand still and point your nose right at it and breathe in all that glorious scent until you can't take any more and the bird bursts into the sky and then you get told you're a good boy and get pats and cuddles. The Boss Man seems to know when all that's starting to happen and usually distracts me before I get too carried away. I'd really like to be able to do it again though but might have to wait until I go back to the hot dry place again.

When we're outside I'm always on a lead attached to the clippy thing around me, but there's a place with big walls around it where we take it off and play Silly Boy. I run around in circles really fast and the people laugh so I run some more and then bounce around them. Sometimes they throw a ball away so I bring it back to them but then they throw it away again! It's mad but great fun.

I'm having such a lovely time here, but the people don't seem to know my name as nobody calls me "Fritz". I hear what sounds like "jak-sunn" a lot but don't know what that means. I don't mind that they don't know my name though. They get lots of other stuff right.

I'm sending you a picture from outside today so you can see how smart I look. Hare is very well but someone did something to HedgePig and he's not very well sadly.

I'll write again soon.

Your friend

Fritz

27th March 2021

Dear Milo

Well, what a day it's been!

The Boss Man disappeared off early, dressed in some strange looking (and smelling!) trousers and boots, and didn't come back for ages. When he did come back, he smelled amazing - lots of things I knew and lots of things I didn't. One of the strange ones reminded me of the blanket I sleep on, a little bit.

Then we went for a long, long walk through the fields and it was wonderful. I had a different lead on today and I was able to run a long way away from the Boss Man (but never TOO far, though) and spend ages snoofering around on the grass and in bushes before running back to him. I got to play in a muddy ditch and roll on my back in the long grass, although sadly I couldn't find anything particularly smelly to roll in. And then we met Ella and her person. Ella is a young Welsh Otterhound who lives very close to where I'm staying. And she didn't have a lead on!! She's very hairy and reminds me of Silver and the other wire-haired boys and girls at home. I was excited to see her so put my chin on the ground and my bum in the air and asked her to play. She started running so I chased her and then she chased me and then I chased her again and then she knocked me over! That's never happened before, but then she is bigger and heavier than me. Sadly she had to go then, and so did we so we finished our walk and went back to the house.

The Boss Man seemed very happy and kept telling me what a good boy I was. Every now and again we'd stop and he'd give me something lovely to eat, but that only seems to happen when my bum is on the ground, for some reason. I was so tired afterwards I went to bed immediately after my lunch and didn't move for ages.

Later we got into the car and went to a place called "The Yard". It's a very busy place with lots of buildings and a big open bit and a huge big sandpit and another smaller sandpit in a big shed and lots of people. The people all seemed to know who I am even though we've never met before and I got lots of strokes and cuddles, but the Boss Man kept checking I was ok and wasn't getting scared. They all kept making that "jak-sunn" sound so it obviously means something. I'm determined to get to the bottom of it.

And then I met someone very important called "Uncle Reefing" who lives at The Yard. Uncle Reefing is a horse and brown. He's absolutely ginormous and a bit scary when you first meet him but he's kind and gentle and very wise. He and the Boss Man have been friends for a terribly long time - he shouts when he sees the Boss Man and the Boss Man reaches up to give him the biggest cuddles ever and calls him his "Big Fella". A long time ago they used to go from place to place and jump over things together which sounds a bit odd but I don't know much about that. I didn't get to talk much with Uncle Reefing as he was about to have his tea, but he did tell me I've really landed on my paws. I don't know what that means, but it sounds really clever so I probably did it by accident. We gave each other a good sniff to introduce ourselves.

We went for another walk then, near the yard. It was another exciting place and I found a lovely smelly thing that used to be a bird but wasn't allowed to investigate it properly which made me sad. Afterwards we went to see Uncle Reefing again but he was busy eating dry grass so the Boss Man gave him a last cuddle and off we went.

It was such a busy and full day that I can't keep my eyes open so I'm off to bed now. I really hope I have another day like it soon.

Your friend

Fritz

P.S. Hare had a little accident but the Boss Lady helped her and she's all better now. HedgePig is still unwell, and I can't find Phezzie.

P.P.S. I've realised what the smell on my blanket reminds me of - it's Uncle Reefing!!

28th March 2021

Dear Milo

I don't know when I'm going back, but I really don't want this holiday to end. It's amazing to think that only seven sleeps ago I was up in the air with all those other dogs, not knowing where we were going or what was going to happen to us. I hope everyone else is having as nice a time as I am. I'm sure they are.

I went in the car again today with the Boss Man. He has to lift me into it, as my bum isn't bouncy enough to get me up that high yet. I think with all the walking and games of Silly Boy it won't be long until I'm able to do it myself though but until then it's like an extra-big cuddle every time. When we got to The Yard we said hello to Uncle Reefing. He told me the first thing I need to know about The Yard is to be careful where I stand. He says he doesn't know where his own feet are half the time, never mind mine, and he doesn't want me to get hurt. He has big pieces of metal stuck on them and they make a lot of noise when he walks into his house.

I also met Lola, who owns The Yard. She is fierce and brave and loyal and fierce. Yes, she's extra-fierce. As a miniature dachshund she's only little but I don't think anyone has told her that and anyway that's only on the outside. Inside, she's a huge big dog. She has decided we're going to be friends and says she's going to look after me and show me some rope. If anyone gives me any trouble I'm to tell her and she'll sort them out. We played for ages on the grass until her person - a tall man with a face like a wirehaired - picked her up. This made her very cross and she wriggled until he had to put her back on the ground again. She got very excited about the whole thing - maybe even more excited than me! The tall man made those odd "Jak-sunn" noises again while he patted me and said I was a Good Boy. I'm sure I'll work it out.

We said goodnight to Uncle Reefing before we left and he called the Boss Man something strange - "Dad". I'm not sure I understand that word but it seems to be very special.

When we got back, the Boss Lady gave me a really yummy new treat that I hadn't tasted before and I saw that it was a present from Lola, which was lovely. Hopefully I'll see her again before I go so I can say thank you. I liked the treat so much that I didn't eat it straight away and tried to hide it in my bed, but the blanket wouldn't stay on top of it which was very annoying. The Boss Lady and the Boss Man seemed to find it very funny, but I wasn't laughing.

I have a new blanket which is ok but it's a bit sad as the last one was just getting to the point where it smelled really good. At least the new one also smells of Uncle Reefing which makes me feel safe and happy.

Hare remains well, though sadly HedgePig isn't getting any better. In fact, he may be getting worse so I'm giving him special attention. Phezzie has also reappeared so that's a relief.

I really enjoy telling you my stories, Milo, so thank you for being my friend. I hope we get to meet soon before I have to leave.

Your good friend

Fritz.

The girl next door – Huge news – The importance of Names

1st April 2021

Dear Milo

I've just met the girl next door and she's gorgeous!

Her name is Rosie. She's a bit younger than me and a Golden Retriever. I tried not to come across too pushy but couldn't help trying to impress her by bringing over some of my toys. She says she likes me because I'm a gentleman, unlike some of the other dogs she meets who "are only interested in one thing". She mentioned someone named Bertie the Boxer who sounds like a right ruffian.

She certainly likes to play, though, and doesn't hold back. That's the second time in a week that I've been knocked over by a girl.

I also noticed that she puts her bottom on the floor a lot when she's with her people. The man with her sounds very odd, but a little bit like the Boss Lady. Rosie says he's "Northern". I think the Boss Lady might be a little bit Northern too, so that's OK. Neither sounds anything like the Boss Man though, who is something called "Irish". I think he sounds fantastic.

I've started sitting on my bottom too. The Boss Lady says the word "sit", I put my bottom on the ground, and I get a treat - it's brilliant! I've also noticed that the people make the "Jak-sunn" noises more when they're looking at me or cuddling me, so it's definitely got something to do with me, whatever it is.

I have to go now as Rosie might be coming over again - I'm going to wait at the gate in any case - but I'll write again soon. Hare has had a little more surgery as something unknown happened to her ear but she's fine now. I think scars add character, anyway. HedgePig remains stable thankfully, and Phezzie has disappeared again.

Your friend

Fritz

5th April 2021

Dear Milo

I have news. Big news. Huge news. The hugest of huge news.

I'm not going back to the other place. I'm going to stay here always and forever, and I couldn't be happier!

I went to The Yard today and was telling Uncle Reefing about the Lovely Lady who took care of me when I was very hungry and said that even though I missed her I would be sad when the time came to go back. He looked at me with his big wise eyes and told me what I'd secretly been hoping since I got here - I'm going to stay and live with the Boss Man and the Boss Lady. The Lovely Lady showed them my picture when I lived far away with her and they decided there and then that they were going to give me a home and love me and care for me forever. Of course, I have a job to do as well. I'm going to love them and take care of them forever too.

I told Uncle Reefing how happy I was but that I'm also a little bit worried. What if I get it wrong again? What if they decide they don't like me or the things I do anymore and send me away? I've had a wonderful time here and love them very much but sometimes I forget and do things without meaning to. Like when I smell birds and run and run and don't hear the Boss Man when he calls to me. Sometimes I get scared and don't like going into the room that's hot and smells of food, especially when things are popping and crackling in there. And then there's the room with the hot flickery smoky orange thing and the big window with people and animals and all kins of noisy stuff in it. I don't like that room at all, even though the Boss Man and the Boss Lady stay there a lot. I've also had a bit of a bark at some things and I know people don't like that.

Uncle Reefing said that if I only knew some of the things he's done to the Boss Man over the years I wouldn't worry at all. He told me they want me to stay with them because I'm special and the things I do make me that way. They will help me get things right so I stop being scared and I stay happy all the time.

I'm going to do my best, Milo. I'm going to make some mistakes, but I'll always try to do what I think they're asking me to do, even if it scares me a bit.

Hopefully I'll get to meet you soon, Milo. Maybe you can come and visit me at my home.

My home.

Your friend

Fritz

12th April 2021

Dear Milo

Well, it HAS been an interesting week! First of all, what on earth is all this white stuff that's falling out of the sky?? It's strange but I'm not entirely sure I like it. It makes my nose very cold when I sniff it.

Anyway, I've been doing some of the same stuff and some new stuff since I last wrote. I have this "Sit" thing nailed. They say the word and my bum's glued to the floor. I've noticed something, though. I don't ALWAYS get a treat when I do it, but it happens often enough that it's worth a go. In fact, I tried looking at them and putting my bum on the floor even before they said anything but nothing happened, sadly. Have you ever had the straight chewy things that look like sticks, by the way? I've tried them but it seems to end up with the world falling out of my bottom so I'm not allowed them anymore.

Walks have become very interesting. I'm getting used to having a run on the extra-long lead, and I've discovered I can get a looooong way away from the Boss Man before I have to stop. I've also been hearing the Boss Man voice a bit more, but I don't think that's connected. I had a great time on Saturday when I found two pheasants, showed the Boss Man where they were and then made them fly! The Boss Man was rubbish at getting through the hedge to join me, though. He definitely needs to work on that. Uncle Reefing tells me I need to be careful. He says you haven't finished the course until you've cleared the last fence, so I shouldn't get too cocky. I'm not sure what that means, but I think he's saying I'm still learning what life here is all about so I should try to take my time and stick close to the Boss Man and Boss Lady.

It's not easy though, when it's early and the ground is damp and that smell rises to my nose making everything else disappear while I follow and follow and follow and follow until I find the birds and make them fly because that's what good boys do, isn't it? I know I'm not supposed to do it all the time, but I find it really hard not to.

We've been playing so much Silly Boy this week! There's a big field outside one of the doors where there are some trees and Boss Lady digs and sticks things in the ground. I'm not allowed to help though. She uses the SERIOUS Boss Lady voice if that happens, so I don't do that anymore. Instead I play with my rope. I run around and around and they throw my rope away and then I run after it really fast and pick it up and then run back really fast again. Sometimes I give the rope back and sometimes I jump around and shake my head and throw it myself. And you know the best thing? I can do all this without any lead at all!!! I wear my clippy strappy thing but other than that I can run around as much as I like without tripping over rope or getting tangled or anything. It's brilliant! There's a big thick hedge on one side that I can't see through, but on the other side is some wire and on the other side of that is Rosie! We've had a great time running up and down. I've noticed that when I'm with

Rosie, the people use the "Jack-sunn" sounds when they're looking at me, but not at her, though. Curious.

I really love it here, Milo. I'll never forget the Lovely Lady who helped me when I needed it, but I feel like this is where I'm supposed to be. The Boss Man and Boss Lady aren't perfect, but I can't expect them to get everything right first time. They need to adjust and learn and we need to remember how new this is to them and how confusing things must be sometimes. I'm going to be patient and cuddle them and love them and help them find their way to make this the best home in the world.

Hare is in very good spirits but doesn't smell as good as she did. She went away for a while and then spent some time on the hot white thing on the wall and now smells like flowers. I'm working hard to fix her though. Phezzie was a good substitute for a while, and HedgePig's nose fell off all by itself.

Good night Milo. Sleep well, and I hope you meet some bunnies in your dreams.

Your friend,

Fritz

18th April 2021

Dear Milo

I've got it! Those "Jax-unn" noises all the people are making? That's me! That's my new name!

I realised this week that the Boss Man and Boss Lady only said it when they were talking to me, and I got lots of treats and cuddles if I looked at them when they said it and they got really excited if I went over to them when they said it so the only conclusion was that it's my name. My name is Jackson. I'm Jackson. I've had a few names in my time, but this one feels like it's really me and I'm going to have it forever.

Uncle Reefing knew all along, of course, but he says it was very important that I work it out for myself and looked very proud of me when I told him. He says names are important because they don't just say who we are, but where we come from and who we can be too. He's named after his grandfather who came from a faraway place called America a long time ago. He was very famous for running really really fast and was faster than any other horse in the world until he had an accident. His people helped him then and although he couldn't run fast anymore he had a long and happy life afterwards. Uncle Reefing is very proud of his grandfather but he did a different thing with his life and jumps over things as well as just running.

Hearing about Uncle Reefing's grandfather made me a bit sad, because I never knew my grandfather, or even my father. Then he told me something amazing. He told me where my name came from:

When the Boss Man was just a pup, his family lived with a Pointer just like me. His name was Pollock. There's a story behind his name too, but apparently that's for another day. Anyway, Pollock was a Very Good Boy and loved the Boss Man's father very much. His job was to look after the Boss Man and his family and take care of them and make sure no harm came to them, as well as finding birds. And he did all this until he was very very old and had to go away. The Boss Man loved Pollock and never forgot him and that's why he had been looking for me. There was a man in America called Jackson Pollock who was very famous for drawing pictures and the Boss Lady figured that if I was called Jackson, we could put my name and Pollock's name together and make his name! Apparently the man's pictures were very messy so I think I can do that too.

That made me very happy. Uncle Reefing also said that because I've been adopted I can now choose who I want as my family. I've been thinking about that and have decided that I'm going to adopt Pollock as my grandad. I'm going to try to be like him and look after my family forever and ever but still be proud of where I've come from.

I've been learning more stuff this week. Now that I know my name I'm getting better at going over to my people when they say it but, to be honest, the possibility of getting some cheese means I'm probably going to give it a go even if they say somebody else's name. I've been allowed back on the long rope again after the unpleasantness last week and I was a Very Good Boy today. I also spent a lot of the week helping the Boss Man with his work, but a lot of his work is just sitting talking to people in a little box so it's quite boring. My job is to make it less boring, and I'm very good at it. The people in the box make lots of excited noises when I look them and even when I'm asleep the Boss Man pokes me now and again, especially when I'm enjoying a really good snore. It's tough work, but we do what we can.

I've met lots of other dogs this week, including a wire-haired pointer. She didn't really want to talk to me though. I also met Bertie the Boxer! He wasn't as much of a ruffian as Rosie said, and was very friendly. He only has a short little tail, but I could hardly see it as it was wagging so fast. He's very strong, but quite young and I think most of his growing has gone into his muscles instead of his brain. He was with two Rhodesian Ridgeback ladies who didn't want to play at all. This evening I played in the garden with Rosie again but she got told off. I was Very Good.

It has been lovely and warm - almost like the place I came from - so I've been spending a lot of time outside sunbathing. I thought Hare would like it too but I wasn't allowed to bring her outside. When the Boss Lady wasn't looking though I brought HedgePig out so he could hibernate in the bushes. He didn't like it and his nose fell off again and lots of weird stuff came out. Boss Lady took him away and when he came back he was good as new! Almost.

I must go now as there is a thing for me to bark at. Thank you for being my friend.

Your friend

Jackson

25th April 2021

Dear Milo

Thank you for your letter. It was lovely to hear from you and nice to see that I'm not alone in having problems with training my people that there's no difference between inside and outside toys and life's too short to worry about muddy feet. Not that there's been much mud in the last week though - all this sunshine reminds me of the place I lived before coming here!

I've had another busy week. One day the Boss Man didn't spend his time talking to the people in the box but instead spent the whole day outside with me, which was wonderful. We went on long walks in new places and he actually tried to run at one point, which was almost as funny as seeing his legs in the first place. He didn't last long although, to be fair, I will admit that I was quite tired that evening too and slept very well.

Yesterday we went in the car but instead of going to The Yard, the Boss Man, Boss Lady and I went to a very smart town where people sit on narrow bits of wood and push themselves up and down the river for some strange reason. Anyway, it turns out we were going to see the V.E.T. so it was probably just as well that I didn't know. The V.E.T. was very nice but I didn't want to go with her at first and was a bit scared until Mum came to the door with me. Then everything was ok and I knew I was safe.

I met lots of new people who all told me how handsome I am and what a Good Boy I am, although I was prodded and poked a lot and had a needle stuck in me and some blood taken out which I thought was a bit rude.

As I thought, I'm very fit and healthy and putting on weight. I'm heavier than I was when I arrived and will have reached my target weight when I've put on another little bit. Most of me is muscle though, so I'm still quite lean. Luckily the Lovely Lady who looked after me in the other place took such good care of me that the V.E.T. already knew most of what they needed to know before I even got there. I liked all the people I met but was very glad to get out and see the Boss Man and Boss Lady when we were done.

After we got home (Home. I still love that) we went for another walk to someplace nearby but different. There was a river there which was great fun, but the people didn't want to come in, which was their loss. After we got back and played a lot of Silly Boy, the Boss Man brought me into the room I don't like - you know, the one with the hot thing and the big moving window? I didn't like it but when he sat down on the thing like a big bed on legs I thought that looked safe and got up beside him, which seemed to make him very happy. I spent a little while still keeping an eye out for monsters, but it seemed safe enough first to lie down and then safe enough for a little snooze. But Milo, the cuddles! We were there for ages and ages and the Boss Man hardly moved apart from stroking my head and my ears - it was wonderful! When I needed to go outside though I got a bit scared again, but I think I might give that room another try.

We had a Very Important Visitor today. I know she was important because the Boss Man and Boss Lady spent ages tidying things and brushing me and putting my toys away. When she arrived she reminded me of the Lovely Lady which was nice but I was a little worried at first she might be there to take me away again so was a bit shy. I didn't need to worry though as she brought presents!! Have you had Sausage Treats Milo? Well these weren't just Sausage Treats - these were special Sausage Treats with carefully selected cuts of Venison and Tripe. Lovely. The VIV is friends with the Lovely Lady and was here especially to see me and make sure I was happy and also to help my people look after me. She lives with lots of Pointers (including two from the same place I lived) and I'm going to go visit and play with them soon. I gave her lots of wags before she left and am looking forward to seeing her again.

The Boss Man and I visited Uncle Reefing at The Yard this evening after he'd had his tea. After cuddles in his house and after the Boss Man had put his pyjamas on, Uncle Reefing and I talked about me and my hunting. I think I'm getting better at listening and try to pay more attention to the Boss Man but it's really hard, especially in places where there are oh so many wonderful-smelling birds. And I'm good at it, Milo. I'm really, really good at finding birds.

Uncle Reefing says that the Boss Man will help me with it. He's going to talk to someone who has taught lots and lots of other dogs to listen and to hunt properly and make their people happy and will get them to teach me too. That will mean that I'll be more like Grandad Pollock and be a Very Good Boy. I'm going to do my very best Milo, and I know Dad will help me and we'll be a great team just like his Dad and Grandad Pollock and like him and Uncle Reefing. I've already started and paid such close attention during our walk this evening and only started hunting a couple of times and stopped when I was asked to.

I have a really good feeling about this Milo. It's going to be wonderful.

Hare remains well, as does Phezzie. HedgePig is in remarkably good spirits, all things considered.

Sleep well my friend. I'm going to find the Boss Man and give the room I don't like another go.

Your friend

Jackson

*A scary time – What not to eat – Adventures
with a mousey – The problem with birds*

3rd May 2021

Dear Milo

I hope you and your people are doing well and staying
warm and dry in this yucky weather. It was so nice and
hot last week; I can't believe I have to have my coat on
again to go out now.

Like the weather, my week has had its ups and downs
too.

I think lots of the dogs like me that come from far away
put on a very brave face when they tell you about their
adventures and only talk about the good things that
happen. They make jokes when things go wrong, but it's
hard, Milo. It's hard work coming to a place that's so
different from what you've always known and trying to fit
in to something you don't really understand. I always try
my best to do what I'm asked and to make the Boss Man
and Boss Lady happy, but I don't always really know
what they want and I often get it wrong. Even when I get
it right it's really hard to do something that's so new to
me and it's often scary and I feel very unsure of myself.
The Boss Man and Boss Lady love me and are there to
help me, but even though they're kind and gentle

sometimes I forget and think they're going to be like the other people before and I get frightened. Like when he was first asking me to do things, the Boss Man used to sometimes lift his hand in the air and that sometimes worried me so I'd run away a little bit and put my tail between my legs. I think he knows I don't like it though because he doesn't do that anymore.

I've been meeting other people too, and I like to take my time to make sure they're nice before I get too close to them. I haven't met any nasty people yet, but I'm still being careful.

I was very unhappy one day. A man came to do something to a machine in the house and the house stopped being warm like it usually is. The Boss Lady sat in one of the rooms that I like and when she turned around there was a flickery hot orange thing in a metal box behind her and I was very frightened of it. I've smelled this thing before and it's very fierce and dangerous. I was too scared to be in the room with it and ran out and stood outside, trying to get the Boss Lady to come out too. She wasn't scared at all though and sat really close to it, talking to the little people in the box for a while. When she saw I was scared, she tried to get me to come back into the room but it was far too terrible to do that, so we both went outside and came back into the house a different way so I didn't have to go past it. When the Boss Man came home the flickery hot orange thing was gone but I could still smell it and the danger was still there. They sat in the room then with Hare and HedgePig and tried to get me to come in. I really wanted to, Milo. I really, really wanted to go in to them but I was so scared. I was so scared, I whined, and then I was so scared and sad and worried about them I cried. I howled, Milo. I howled and howled. I could see them there and I love them and wanted to be with them and protect them and keep them safe but I couldn't because it was so dangerous and I was very very frightened. Dad came out to me then and I could tell he was really sad and unhappy too. He cuddled me lots then and told me I was a Good Boy and then I felt ok and a bit happier.

After a while I tried looking into the room again and it felt a bit safer so I very slowly crept back in, keeping an eye on the metal box where the flickery hot orange thing had been. When I got to Mum she put her arms around me and gave me the biggest cuddles and told me I was a Very Good Boy and I felt very brave. Although I was much happier then, I still thought it best to get Hare and go to my bed for a while. I've been going in and out of the room since then and it's all fine again now. The flickery hot orange thing hasn't come back, but I'll keep watching, just in case.

It hasn't all been bad, though - we've been on lots and lots of walks, and I had a date with Rosie yesterday! The Boss Lady and Boss Man sat in our big place with Rosie's people talking Northern and drinking fizzy water while she and I ran up and down with my rope and with my ball. Rosie is very fast and I think she can run further than I can but I'm getting stronger and faster all the time. I'm eating a lot and sometimes can't finish my dinner (the dry bits anyway - I always eat the chicken!) so I weigh more than I used to. I'm getting better at playing too because although Rosie knocked me over a couple of times, I knocked her over too, for the first time! Rosie loves everyone and will stop and talk to any person she meets. I've told her she needs to be more careful, but I don't think she's met the same kind of people I have. Everyone I've met here has been lovely, but I remember what happened before when people are mean even if you do your best so I'm still being careful.

I had a fantastic time today at The Yard where I got to play with Lola and then went for a run in the place where Uncle Reefing and his best friend Wilf (who is also a horse, but orange) eat grass all day. It was amazing! I had the clippy strappy thing on with the really long rope and Dad let me put my nose down and sniff and sniff and run wherever I wanted without telling me to stop at all. The smells were wonderful - birds and bunnies and worms and beetles and mouses and more bunnies and Uncle Reefing and all kinds of things. I ran and ran and found lots of things and whenever I stopped and looked at Dad he told me I was a Good Boy. Sometimes I had to stop suddenly because the rope wasn't long enough but most of the time I stuck pretty close to Dad so that was ok.

I found some Pheasants though and really wanted to catch them so that was the hardest bit. I was really good at finding them - I smelled them a little bit, and then a bit more, then a bit more and followed and followed and followed and followed and followed and then there they were! I could smell them in the long grass, really really close and pointed at them to tell Dad exactly where they were. Then one of them moved a little bit and I moved too and they burst into the air and flapped up and up.

There was no big noise though, and they just flew away instead of falling down, but Dad still patted me and told me I was a Good Boy anyway. I think Grandad Pollock would be proud of me.

Today is Uncle Reefing's birthday! He's 24. I don't know how much that is but it's lots. Mum brought cake to The Yard but Uncle Reefing didn't want any and I wasn't allowed. The people liked it though. Uncle Reefing says he doesn't mind getting older. He says life isn't a speed class and given the alternative, he's very happy to keep trotting on. I didn't understand any of that. He told me he celebrated his birthday by doing some jumping with the Boss Man this morning. He says when he was younger he used to jump shoes, or something like that. It doesn't sound very hard, to be honest, but I didn't say anything because it's his birthday and I was being polite. Maybe I'll try some of this shoe-jumping when the weather is nicer. The Boss Lady has loads and I'm sure she won't mind lending me one.

I also had a lovely time last night, when I was with the Boss Man in the place where he talks to the people in the box all day. There's a big soft bed on legs there too, and he was sitting on it when I decided all on my own that I wanted to be on it too so I jumped up to be with him. He made a big fuss of me then so I snuggled down with my head on his knees and enjoyed the cuddles until I fell asleep. Dad stayed with me looking at a square paper thing and he was still there when I woke up, with his hand on my head. I felt so loved and safe and happy, Milo. Is this what home means?

I'm here to stay, in any case. This is where I live and The Boss Man and Boss Lady and Uncle Reefing are my family. Sometimes it's hard and things go wrong and that makes us unhappy for a little while but most of the time it's wonderful. I know Mum and Dad love me and I'll keep trying to understand what they ask me to do. I'll keep looking after them all and protecting them, and hopefully they'll understand me too. I'm going to do my best anyway.

Have you noticed that I call my people different things at different times? I don't know how that's happened, but it feels right somehow. Maybe it's because they don't want anything from me other than to be me, and to be happy. It doesn't make a difference if I'm good at finding birds for them or not – they will never throw me away.

Hare is very well, as is Phezzie, although he's getting a bit whiffy (and that's me saying this!) so I'm almost hoping the same thing happens to him that happened to Hare a while ago when she went away and came back smelling like flowers. Hedgepig is, as always, HedgePig, though a little quieter since his last surgery.

Goodnight Milo. Keep looking after your people and hopefully we'll see each other soon.

Your Friend

Jackson

9th May 2021

Dear Milo

I hope you and your people are well.

I often think how lucky I am to have you as a friend. You are the only Labradoodle I know, and it's amazing to think that if your mum and the Boss Man hadn't become friends all those years ago we wouldn't even be friends now. I am very much looking forward to meeting you, even though I know Zummerzet is a very long way away. In the meantime Hare will keep me company. I will never forget how kind and welcoming you were to send her to me when I first got here.

I've learned a lot of new things since I last wrote - some of them nice and some of them not nice. One nice thing is that games of Silly Boy go on a lot longer when I give my rope or my ball to Mum or Dad to throw, instead of just running around with it. Sometimes I forget to give it though, and sometimes I try to play Tug rather than hand it over. Mum and Dad don't like it when I do that and stop playing then. Uncle Reefing says that it's because I'm a retriever and I'm not supposed to hold onto things but instead give them over when I'm asked. I do that with Hare and Phezzie and even HedgePig, but it's really hard with fun stuff like balls and rope.

I also learned that some of the things Mum and Dad give me to eat are yummy but disagree with my tummy. They gave me this chewy thing all wrapped up in cheese one day and it was delicious. I swallowed it down in one gulp, and the world was lovely. For a while, anyway. Late that night, Milo, my poor, poor tummy! I really wanted to go outside, but it was very dark and Mum and Dad were both asleep. I wandered around for a little bit until I couldn't hold it in any more and had an unpleasantness. And then a little later it happened again! I was very sad and scared that Mum and Dad would be cross with me when they saw. I didn't need to worry though, because when they DID see, they called me a Poor Boy and gave me big cuddles. I had been feeling sorry for myself but that made me feel a little better. Mum took me outside then, even though I was quite empty, and when we came back everything was all tidy again.

I had a little bit of breakfast and then had a rest-day as I was very tired and my tummy definitely wasn't itself. It took a little while for me to get better, and I saw Mum was talking on the small people-box to a lady that looked very much like the V.E.T. I met a little while ago, although this one was much smaller, obviously. Dad was gone all day and when he got back he put this soft stuff into his hand and then let me lick it off. It was delicious, and I had lots of it for a while but I don't have it any more. I'm feeling much better now, by the way. Back to my old self. Uncle Reefing thinks I had some medicine that went wrong. He says I don't need to worry, and that if I need more medicine in the future, Mum and Dad will make sure it's different and doesn't affect my tummy. I really hope so as I don't want the world to fall out of my bottom again.

I also learned a very important lesson at The Yard, Milo, and if you don't already know this, listen very, very carefully. There are little white ropes that will sting and bite you. I know! Who would have thought it! I was with Dad and on my long lead when I thought I saw a bunny in one of the fields so went to say hello. I did it quite quickly, to be fair, and I think I caught Dad a little bit on the hop. (I hope you liked my bunny joke there). Anyway I crouched down and snuck under this timber thing, and the tip of my tail got bitten by a thin white rope that was attached to it! It didn't hurt that much, to be honest, but I got a terrible shock. I yelped and ran away but stopped and looked back to see Dad galloping after me. I don't know about Uncle Reefing but looking at the way Dad leaped the fence to get to me, I don't think shoe-jumping will have been hard for him at all. I was still a bit nervous when he got near me as I still wasn't sure what had happened, but when he knelt down and opened his arms wide, I ran to him for cuddles and felt a lot better. I was still very cautious when we got back to Uncle Reefing's house though. I didn't even want to play with Lola, so I hope she doesn't think I was being rude. Apparently, the bitey ropes are to stop naughty horses breaking the bits of timber.

Uncle Reefing says that the important thing for me to learn is first, stay away from the little white ropes, and second, that when I need help, Mum and Dad will always be there to give it. He says that while it's brave and strong to try to work things out and fix them yourself, sometimes you need to be even braver and stronger than that and let others help you. He and Mum and Dad and I are a family now, and we must always help each other, even if it's hard. Especially if it's hard.

The last thing I learned is that there are things that look like toys, smell like toys and feel like toys but, and this is the strange bit, aren't toys at all! If you play with these things the people get grumpy and you get the Boss Man or Boss Lady voice. So far I've worked out that some of these things are:

Sleeves

Cushions

My clippy strappy thing

Leads

Towels

Green things in the garden

My coat

Blankets

Frilly things hanging off cushions and blankets

Rolls of soft paper stuff

That last one is, to be honest, probably worth the trouble. I found one in the room where Mum talks on the small people-box when she wasn't there and it was so soft and squishy and little bits came off and then it moved a bit and more came off and it's just the right size to fit between my paws and then more came off and it rolled across the room and then more came off and then Mum came in. I think she was trying to be cross, but she didn't do very well at it. I've looked to see if there are any more of the soft squishy things around but I think they've all been put away now.

In any case, thank you as always for listening, Milo. I'm still learning what it is to be part of a family and this life is still strange to me. I'm learning new things every day and soon it will be like I've always been here. I will never forget where I've come from though. There were some lovely people who helped me when I needed it and someday I hope I'll be able to help them too.

Since we last spoke, Phezzie went off for a little while and came back smelling like flowers, just like Hare did. HedgePig didn't go away and I have discovered that I can fit him almost completely in my mouth, which is nice.

Sleep well, Milo. I'll write again soon.

Your friend

Jackson

16th May 2021

Dear Milo

Thank you for your letter and I hope you have been successful with the "big eyes" method of getting yourself more food. I think I'm now getting a little bit less food than I did at first, but it's still as much as I'm able to eat and I'm still getting heavier. I'm interested in the idea about a second ball though. Let me get this straight; you have a ball, and they have ANOTHER ball. And they throw their ball to trick you into dropping the one you have??!? That makes no sense whatsoever. I didn't even know about balls before I got here and to think there is more than one is amazing!

We have had a lot of excitement here since I last wrote. Before I tell you anything, I have to say that Hare is fine. She's doing very well and sitting here in my bed right now along with Phezzie. HedgePig on the other hand is an entirely different matter.

It was a few days ago that I realised I hadn't seen him for a little while. I looked everywhere for him - in the places I like and even in the places I don't like but couldn't find him. The last thing I remembered was that we were playing outside (even though he's not allowed outside) and he was having a great time. I searched all of outside for him too, but still couldn't find him. HedgePig was lost! It was raining then, so I got very sad thinking about him being cold and wet and all alone in the dark. I wondered if I'd been mean to him and he'd run away and it was all my fault. I remembered his funny little face and the way he squeaked with happiness when I chewed his bottom. I missed him terribly and was very unhappy.

But then! A few sleeps later Mum was outside putting some flowery things in the ground and taking other flowery things out of the ground when she came inside carrying something that looked like a small muddy potato. It was HedgePig! It turns out he accidentally fell into a hole that someone accidentally dug and then had dirt accidentally put on top of him and then someone accidentally forgot where he was.

I was so happy to see him and wanted to play with him straight away but Mum insisted that he had to go into the hot swirly wet thing first and then the hot swirly dry thing before I could see him again. When I did get him back I gave him a big cuddle with my mouth and told him he's NOT an outside toy; he's a very Naughty Boy.

I told Uncle Reefing about what had happened and he said how funny it is that we often don't miss the important ones around us until they're lost. He didn't look like he thought it was funny though. He said that we should make the most of every second we have and that we should make sure that everyone always knows that we love them because we can never tell when somebody is going to be lost. Uncle Reefing seemed really sad so I think he might have lost someone he loved and not found them again. I hope I can make him feel happier by being his friend and taking really good care of HedgePig from now on.

I went out with Dad today in the place where Uncle Reefing and Wilf eat grass all day. I had the really long rope on so could run around all over the place, looking for birds. I could only find the little ones today though - there weren't any pheasants or partridges anywhere, but I still had a great time snorfling in the long grass and the bushes, smelling everything there was to be smelled. I found a lovely smelly thing in one bush but only got a quick mouthful before Dad used the Boss Man voice and I had to leave it.

It's all so different to when I lived in the other place, and that seems like an awfully long time ago. Over there, I was hungry most of the time and very, very thin. You could see all my ribs and my back was all lumpy. I was even a different colour! I didn't live in a nice place like I do now, and I didn't have a comfy cosy bed. The place I lived was made of bits of metal that got hot when the sun was hot and let the water in when the rain fell. The ground was hard and dirty and I had another metal box to sleep in. I'm sending you a picture so you can see what it was like. Most of the time I was tied up so couldn't run and play, but I still had a job. Sometimes The Man would come to give me a little bit of food and sometimes he would take me in a big open car with other men and other dogs and go to the high place. I was let off my rope then and I was able to run around with the other dogs and it was great. Our job was to find birds, show The Man where they were and make them fly. The Man would point a long stick at the birds and it would make a really, really loud noise.

The birds would fall down then, sometimes, and other times they would fly away. If the bird fell down, we had to try to find it. If I did, though, The Man used to shout at me and take the bird away even though I was very hungry. I didn't really understand what he wanted me to do most of the time so I got shouted at a lot and sometimes worse. I worried that I might be a Bad Dog so I always came back to The Man because that's what Good Dogs do. Some of the other dogs didn't come back and either got lost or ran away. I think about them sometimes and hope they're ok. I hope the Lovely Lady who looked after me found them too and got them a new home like mine.

Dad and I also went to a new place one day. As we were coming home from our last walk we passed a house near home. It's a big house with lights outside and a lot of tables on a grassy bit beside it. There were some men sitting at one of the tables and they waved at us and Dad waved back and went over to them. I knew one of the men as he lives with my Spaniel friend Ivy who had puppies a little while ago. I met her the other day and she says the novelty has worn off and she's looking forward to getting her life and her figure back.

Anyway, the men were all drinking big glasses of brown scummy water, and when Dad sat down they gave him one too. This seemed to make him very happy. The men smiled and laughed a lot and didn't really pay much attention to me so I got to give them all a good sniff before asking for cuddles. Two of them smelt like they lived with dogs I knew - Ivy and also Welly, Bonnie and Scrumpy. Another man arrived and he had a big glass of brown scummy water too and then another man came but he had a big glass of wee instead and the rest of the men though this was really funny.

I like this house. The men were nice and left me alone unless I asked them for strokes, and I was able to get onto the seat beside Dad and get mostly into his lap while he talked to his friends. He kept petting me and telling me I was a Good Boy and some of the men said it too. These were nice men and not at all like the men in the other place. I'm not sure yet, but Rosie might be right about people being good. I'm going to take my time and be careful but this is definitely different to what I've seen before.

It's time to say goodnight now, Milo, so I'll finish here. I love my new life and am learning new things every day.

Stay happy and take care of your people.

Your friend

Jackson

23rd May 2021

Dear Milo

I did it, Milo! I did it! All those hours and hours of patience and hard work have paid off and I finally caught a mousey!

In the place behind home with the big walls, there's a little wooden house where Mum puts the things she digs holes with and lots of other things too. I'm not sure exactly what's in there as I'm not allowed in. It smells really odd though - like dirt and wood and bird poo but also this nasty stuff that makes my nose wrinkle. I'd really like to go in there but I get told off if I try so I don't.

Anyway, behind this house and next to the wall is a pile of wood and that's where the mousies live. I knew they were there because I can always smell them and I saw one once. My plan was to sniff very loudly at one end and then run really fast to the other end to catch them as they came out. I spent ages doing this, running to and fro (I believe that once you have a plan you should stick to it) and today one of the mousies ran fro when he should have been running to and ran straight into my mouth!

If I'm honest Milo, I hadn't really planned past this point and wasn't quite sure what to do next so I went to look for Mum to show her how good and clever I was. I couldn't find her though, so eventually put the mousey down on the grass. Then I got a bit distracted and forgot about him a little bit until I heard Mum find him. I think a lot of people heard her find him, actually.

She didn't seem very pleased and appeared more worried about the mousey than she was proud of me as she picked him up and put him in a little box next to the wood so that he could go home. I think the mousey must have been enjoying himself because when he came out of the little box he didn't go back into his house but came outside again! It struck me then that Mum wasn't telling me I was a Good Boy because she hadn't seen me catch the mousey the first time so I caught him again. She still didn't seem happy so I decided I'd hold onto the mousey until Dad got home and show him instead, but she used a very loud Boss Lady voice and I had to give mousey back to her. She put him back in the box and put bits around it so the only way mousey could go was back into the wood pile. I think mousey had a great time. He was fine apart from being a bit soggy and just think of the story he can tell his friends about the time he played with me.

I told Uncle Reefing about my adventure when I went to The Yard and he said that it runs in the family and told me a story about Grandad Pollock. When the Boss Man was small he had a big brown bunny that lived with him. The bunny lived in a little house and ate grass and carrots and stuff. One day the bunny got out of his house and went for a run. Grandad Pollock found him though, and decided the safest thing for the bunny was to bring him to the Boss Man's Dad who would know what to do. So that's what he did. He picked the bunny up in his mouth and trotted off until he found the people and made sure the bunny got home safely. The bunny went back into his house and everyone was happy. Except for the bunny, maybe, as he didn't have the adventure he was expecting and was probably also a bit soggy, like the mousey.

Uncle Reefing says we all have our natures and things we're good at. We should do the things we're good at - him with his shoe-jumping and me with finding birds - and make sure that we do them properly and don't do bad things. People love us as we are and we should never pretend and try to be someone we're not. He says proper pointers have soft mouths and that makes me one of the very best.

We had a man come to visit today. I met him before and he's quite nice but today he actually came inside! Right into where we live! Nobody has ever come into where we live before and I wasn't sure quite what to do so I wagged my tail but still gave a little bit of a woof to let him know I was watching. He wasn't fussed though and kept talking with Mum and Dad and drinking some hot stuff. I figured he was OK after that so gave him a sniff to make sure he was who I thought he was and then he gave me a pat and everything was fine.

I prefer that kind of person, I think. Sometimes people get too excited and want to play and don't give you any space, even when you don't know them. I'm always polite with these people, but I'm happier to take my time and have a proper introduction first.

Do you ever wonder, Milo, what your people think about when we go for walks? I worry sometimes that they get bored, going to the same places all the time. I mean, it's different for us. We have our noses and every time we go outside it's new and exciting. We can tell who's been where and what birds are nearby. We can smell things on the wind that are miles away. We leave each other pee-mails to say how we are and what we're doing so we can catch up on all the local news. I suppose if smellery is the word we use to say what we smell with our noses, you could use the word seenery to describe what people see with their eyes. I really hope they enjoy their walks as much as we do, but still it's good to get them out and about and away from the people-box for a little while.

Hare and Phezzie are fine although even I think Phezzie is quite stinky at the moment. The man today also brought me a new friend called Ducky and he's settling in very well. He and Phezzie are always game. HedgePig is a bit subdued after his recent adventures and I think he's a little jealous of my game with mousey this morning. You could say his nose is a bit out of joint, but that would be mean given his...condition.

So, until next time, Milo, I will say goodnight. Be a Good Boy and the cuddles will come your way.

Your good friend

Jackson

30th May 2021

Dear Milo

I don't often miss the other place I lived before coming to live here, but I still remember how nice and warm it was most of the time. Today really reminded me of how lovely it is to be out in the fresh air, smelling the smells and feeling the sun on your back and the grass tickling your tummy.

Today we had a big adventure and I met a really nice old lady and her people. Her name is Gracie and she's a Border Collie who lives a long way away. Mum put lots and lots of bags into the car - my water bowl and leads and food bowl and water and treats and poo bags and food - and then we went and drove for ages. I was very good and just snoozed in the back but looked out now and again to see the people behind us. Gracie lives in a place with lots of ups and downs whereas where I live is more an along kind of place. She's very very old and can't see or hear terribly well, so spends most of the time going "What?" very loudly. She's very kind though and let me borrow her toys and we played a little bit but gently. She knows Mum and Dad and was very pleased to see them once she realised who they were. Mum and Dad used to take care of her a long time ago when she was younger and her people went on holiday for a little while.

We went for a walk which was very exciting as there were lots of new things for me to see and sniff. Most of the time we were going up but there was a short bit of very down at the end. Gracie walks very slowly and wasn't able to get down so her Dad carried her. He carries her a lot. I think it's his way of telling her he loves her even though he pretends to grumble about it. There were lots and lots of birds that I could smell, but Dad had put the short lead on my clippy strappy thing and wouldn't let me go near where they were sitting down so I didn't make them fly.

When we got back to Gracie's house there were more people there and although we were outside I got a little bit worried as there was a lot of talking and laughing and moving around a big table. There was also a very little person with wiggly feet who made a surprising amount of noise for someone so small. Dad and I sat on the grass for a little bit so I could have a good look at them all and then he brought me back. I didn't really like it but I first sat down and then lay down beside his chair as he kept stroking me and then it was all OK. I knew I was safe because I was with my people and if my people were happy then I was happy too. We were there for ages, and Mum and Dad kept checking with me to see if I wanted anything but I was happy to stay with them.

Every now and then I'd climb halfway onto Dad's lap just to remind everyone how good and clever I am.

Gracie is a very nice old lady and I'm glad I met her (even though I think she thought I was her great-nephew or something), but I was ready to go home in the end. Hare had come with me and kept me company all the way home. That's the longest trip I've had since I moved here and it was fun. I hope my next trip is as nice.

I'm afraid the bird-finding went to my head again the other day. We were out for a walk and it was a perfect day for looking for birds; the ground was cool but the sun was out and the smell was just hanging there over the grass like a golden thread connecting me to another world. I couldn't do anything else except follow and follow and follow and could see and hear nothing else. Even when Dad used his loudest Boss Man voice I couldn't hear him. Even when he stood right in front of me I couldn't see him. Every part of me wanted to - had to - find the birds and make them fly.

In the end, the Boss Man held my collar and took off the long rope and attached the short lead instead. I knew he was unhappy with me but this was the only part of my old life that made me happy and once I start doing it I can't stop myself. Am I a Bad Dog? I don't want to be a Bad Dog and I worry that Mum and Dad will stop loving me if I keep looking for birds but I don't know what else to do. I don't want to mess this up and be sent away.

Uncle Reefing tells me not to worry. He says we all have things that we need to work through and if we trust the people around us to help us, everything will be fine. He also says that Mum and Dad will never give up on us, no matter what we do or how much we frustrate them. Apparently he had a bit of a wild youth himself and has dumped both of them many times in many places. I don't really know what that means but he seemed to be very happy thinking about the memory so I didn't like to ask. I hope he's right though - he has been about everything else so far.

Dad certainly helped me out the other day, and taught me lots of new words in the process! The sun was shining so he got his legs out, which is never not funny. He was attached to me with the long rope and I was having a great time snorfling through the long grass looking for birds (but still listening to him, mind you). Where we walk there is a great smelly muddy bit of water at the bottom of two down bits and sometimes there are duckies to find there. I was following a bird who happened to go down the down bit into the water so I did the same and then the bird went up the up bit at the other side so I did that too. Usually that's OK because Dad then calls me and I turn around and go back to him because, well, you know, cheese.

This time though the clever bird went through a bush at the top of the up bit and I couldn't go back! I couldn't go forward either and I couldn't turn around. I heard Dad behind me say some new words I hadn't heard before and then after a little while some thrashing about, some more words, a splash, LOTS of very loud words, more thrashing, and another splash. It was quiet then for a little bit, and I could tell Dad was Having a Think. Suddenly there was a lot more thrashing and words and next thing Dad was standing in front of me. He took hold of my clippy strappy thing and pulled and then I was free! I was very happy to see him although I think he struggled a bit more with the scratchy things and the stingy things than I did.

I was a little bit worried that he'd be cross with me but he just seemed happy I was OK. We decided we'd both had enough excitement for one morning and went straight home, although Dad's feet made funny squishy noises for ages as he walked. I checked over his legs afterwards but there was no permanent damage apart from the smell. Mum thought it was all very funny but carefully put some white stuff on which seemed to make things better.

So that's what I've learned, Milo. Ask for help and it will come. Your people will do whatever it takes to keep you safe and happy, so we should do that for them too.

Hare is very well and enjoyed her trip today. Phezzie can't decide whether he wants to live inside or outside at the moment. I'm blaming Ducky - he's been a bad influence since he arrived but I'm being very patient with him. They would both do well to learn from HedgePig who has been very well behaved since The Incident.

Anyway, it's been a very long day and Dad is snoring already so it's time for me to go to bed too. Be a Good Boy Milo, and maybe my next trip can be to see you!

Your friend

Jackson

6th June 2021

Dear Milo

I hope you and your people are well and you're being a Good Boy.

Sometimes it seems like I've always been here and sometimes it seems like it was only yesterday I was tied up and always hungry. I thought about that today, as I sat on Dad's lap, trying to eat the cheese from his dinner even though I'd just finished my own. He tried to use the Boss Man voice to stop me but I used the big eyes trick (thanks for that) and made him laugh instead. Then I wiped dribble all over his legs. I really like it here.

The searching for birds is getting better. I still get very excited when I smell them, but Mum and Dad help me a lot. We do two things on our walks now. We do "Wait" where they say the word and I'm supposed to stop and stay where I am until they come to me. I'm really good at it but sometimes I get bored waiting and wander off a bit so they have to remind me. There's often cheese when they get to me though, so it's worth hanging about. We also do "Come" where they say the word and I'm supposed to stop what I'm doing and run over to them. I'm not as good at this one, really. It's very easy to get distracted and veer off toward something far more interesting when you're halfway back. We're getting there, I think, although I was very good and found a lovely pheasant today.

I met lots of dogs since I last wrote. Rosie actually came into the house and ran off with Ducky! I know Uncle Reefing says we should share, but that's a bit much. Mum got him back though and Rosie got told off again but I'm not sure it got through to be honest. I'm beginning to see why Bertie the Boxer fancies her. I saw Lola today at The Yard. She was seeing off a German Shepherd who was lucky Lola only has little legs. I was busy at the time cooling off in Uncle Reefing's water bucket. I couldn't fit completely so only paddled in it with my front legs.

I also met another pointer, but in Dad's people box! I was helping Dad with his work when the lady in the box got very excited and ran off only to come back a few moments later with a black and white pointer named Jack! Jack's father is a wire-haired so he has a little beard. He's only young but was very nice and I hope to meet him some day so we can have a play.

I've also met two other dogs that bother me a bit. One is Sky Dog who lives above the room where Mum works. The room has a window in the roof over Mum's people box and you can see the sky and the clouds when you look up. That reminds me. Bertie told me dogs can't look up. He then got distracted by a big bird in a tree over his head...

Anyway, Sky Dog is never there during the day but when it's dark and you look up there he is, upside down and looking down at you! It's all very disturbing so I usually give a bit of a woof to warn my people that he's about. The other one is Door Dog. Door Dog lives in a shiny door on the side of the place we live. He only moves when I do and although he looks like he woofs when I do, he doesn't make any noise. Very odd. Like Sky-Dog, he's incredibly handsome and you can only see him when it's dark outside.

I was very good at my job of looking after Mum the other day. She was digging in the place with the walls (I was helping) when she fell over and hurt her paw. Dad was away and Mum was in trouble so I immediately ran over to her and sat on my bottom beside her. I was a Very Good Boy and didn't move a muscle until she was ok and able to get up. Then I helped her go inside where she sat down and used some of Dad's words. She's ok but her paw is now almost the same colours as mine and very fat.

Ducky was traumatised by his episode with Rosie but I'm hoping it might scare him into behaving. Hare is fine, but I'm worried that Phezzie is overdoing it as he's looking a little tired. It may be the heat. HedgePig has started to wander again. I found him outside on the grass so he obviously hasn't learned from his past experience.

It has been a quiet time here, and that's nice. I've met more people and that's good but I love spending my time with Mum and Dad or snoozing in the sunshine. Although sometimes I get a little bit worried by some things, I love my home.

My Home.

I still find it amazing that a little while ago I didn't even have one.

Sleep well, Milo. Dream of big bones.

Your friend

Jackson

13th June 2021

Dear Milo

I hope you are well and not finding the sunshine too hot. I know it's quite hard when you're not used to it like I am.

Some very odd things have happened since I last wrote. One day I was snoozing on the grass in the place with the big walls when I heard a loud squawk in the sky. I opened my eyes to see a big shadow go by and then THUMP - a partridge landed on the grass in front of me. Well, most of a partridge anyway. How he managed to get to me without a head I'll never know. Then I remembered. SkyDog! It must have been a present from SkyDog! As you know, when you're a good hunting dog and you find a bird, you must bring it to your people. I'd never found one quite like this before though and wasn't sure if it counted. Mum heard my present arrive too though, so she's looking after it for me until I need it. I went looking for SkyDog in the tree afterwards to say thank you but he wasn't there.

I did find the partridge's head a little later but Mum wouldn't let me keep it which was very unfair. I think one of those big birds with the sharp claws and big hooked beaks took it in the end. Rosie says it was one of them that dropped it in the first place, but I know it was SkyDog.

I was out walking Dad the other day when we met a small dog I didn't know. I wanted to be friends but he started barking at me, telling me I shouldn't be here and that this place isn't for me. He said Mum and Dad should have helped a dog that didn't come from far away like me and that I'm living in a home that should belong to someone else. I tried to tell him the terrible things that happen to dogs like me where I was before - that if you don't have people and nobody loves you then a man comes and takes you away and you never come back. He didn't listen to me though. I could smell that he was angry, but also scared which made me sad. I don't want to scare anyone.

When I told Uncle Reefing he was sad too. He says that if someone needs help then we should do what we can to help them even if they're very far away. Sometimes the ones far away need help more than the ones nearby and sometimes it's the other way around, and helping one doesn't mean we can't help the other. He also says that the ones who complain about who we help often end up not helping anyone at all.

Uncle Reefing told me I fit perfectly into our family as we all come from somewhere else apart from him! He was born only a little way away from The Yard and has lived here all his life. His very famous grandad came from a place called America though and had to go up in the air to get here a long time ago. His mum also came from far away. Grandad Pollock came from a place called Germany (like in my name) to live with Dad and his family. Dad lived a long way away and had to go up in the air to get here too. Mum came from a long way away too, even though she didn't have to go up in the air. I'm happy that I fit in so well here.

I hope I meet that dog again. I'd like to be his friend and show him that he doesn't need to be afraid just because I'm not like him.

I am enjoying the sunshine very much, however! It reminds me of the nice things where I was before although the grass is much nicer here. Mum and Dad aren't managing very well though. They keep trying to do things while the sun is up high, when everybody knows that you're supposed to be snoozing in the shade when that happens. I'm happy to share my pool with them, however. Yes, I have my own pool! It is lovely and I can get in and splash about and stick my nose in the cool, clear water and have a drink if I want to. Rosie came over for a pool party the other day, but she has a cough now and I won't be able to see her for a while. Bertie has a cough too but I'm sure that's just a coincidence. I feel fine and don't have a cough but I'm not allowed to talk to any other dogs for a little while. Uncle Reefing doesn't like too much sun either and comes into his house when it's really hot. He and his friend Wilf dress up in these big white sheets and scary masks to scare bitey flies away when they go outside. I think they look like ghosts and I don't like it.

I'm a little bit worried about Hare. She looks tired so might have to go for a rest soon. HedgePig is losing weight so Mum might need to feed him up too. Phezzie and Ducky are fine, but I think Ducky knows how to open doors. I held him up to the way out yesterday and it opened all by itself. He hasn't managed to do it again since, but I'll keep trying.

It's time for dinner so I'm going to sign off now, Milo. I think your Mum and my Dad are going to arrange for us to meet really soon and I can't wait to see you!

Your friend.

Jackson

21st June 2021

Dear Milo

What on earth is going on with the weather here?!? I mean, where I was before wasn't great, but at least it was warm when it's supposed to be warm and a bit less warm at other times and you didn't have a b-a-t-h every time you stepped outside! Since I got here, it's been wet, cold, warm, very cold, very hot, very wet, very hot again, and now it's cold and wet again. Dad and I went for a walk the other day through the long grass and he started using the special words again as his legs changed colour and his feet started to make funny squishy noises. I just wanted to get home to my blanket but had to stand on a fluffy thing just inside the house and have my paws rubbed and rubbed before I was allowed go back to my bed.

Anyway, I hope you are well and warm and dry. Are Labradoodles waterproof? I think someone told me that but it may have been Bertie, so... I haven't seen him recently because of his cough but hopefully we'll go for a walk together soon. He's not very bright, but he's my friend and a Good Dog.

I've been very brave. When it was cold, the hot flickery smoky thing appeared again in the room I don't like. I could see it through the door and was very worried about Mum and Dad as they sit really close to it and don't seem to realise how dangerous it is. I didn't run away though. I stayed and watched them to make sure they were safe. That's what Good Dogs do, isn't it? We stay even though we're scared and look after our people and keep them safe. The flickery thing went away after a while but I'm going to keep an eye out in case it comes back.

I haven't seen Rosie recently, but we have had a woof over the fence. Her cough is much better and it won't be long before we can meet and play together again. It has been hard not being able to see her but it's what we must do to make sure we keep each other safe. I haven't been talking to other dogs since she told me about her cough either. I'm fine and don't have a cough but I would feel terrible if I carried Rosie's cough and gave it to someone else. It's not much to ask that we take care and think about keeping others safe by staying away from them for a little while. Very soon we'll all be able to go for walks and run and play together again so we need to be patient for just a little longer.

I had a lovely run with Dad in Uncle Reefing's field today and found a partridge but this one had his head attached and flew away. I was very good and went back to Dad when he called me. Most of the time. Well, some of the time anyway. Uncle Reefing doesn't look like a ghost anymore and now wears a raincoat like mine except a different colour and much, much bigger. He doesn't like getting wet and when it's very wet he stays in his house and eats dry grass all day while he talks to his friends about his adventures when he was young. He's older than anyone else at The Yard so knows more than any of them and they all listen to him.

I'm thinking about taking up a new job and quite like the idea of being a Search and Rescue dog. Search and Rescue dogs search for things that are lost and find them and rescue them. I did my first mission the other day. Dad wears these things on his face in front of his eyes and gets wobbly and bumps into things if he doesn't. Somehow, he lost them and had to wear other ones that were the same but very dark and looked very silly and the little people in his people-box laughed at him. Anyway, I was showing Hare the best place to cool off in the flowery things under the big tree when I found them and showed Mum! She said I was Good Boy and then Dad said I was a Very Good Boy when he got home too. I actually found them very close to where the partridge I got from SkyDog landed so I think SkyDog may have had Dad's face nose things too.

I have some bad news about Ducky I'm afraid. We were playing today and suddenly when I wasn't touching him and wasn't even there actually his wing came away and some stuff came out. It was the same kind of stuff that I saw when HedgePig had his first accident, so I'm hoping Mum will be able to help him. I was very worried about him and kept checking on him by jumping up to see as Mum kept him elevated above her head in the recovery position while she took him inside. I'll let you know how he gets on.

It's a little bit lonely right now, Milo, as I miss my friends. I'm glad I can write to you and share my stories, so thank you for listening and thank you for being there. I think we'll meet really soon.

Be good.

Your friend

Jackson

27th June 2021

Dear Milo

Terrible news! I have The Cough!!

It's actually not too bad. I coughed a few times over a couple of days and I've been just fine since then. It was definitely The Cough though – lots of wheezing and then a big old yack. Rosie feels very guilty for giving it to me, but it's not her fault. She hadn't started coughing when we last met, even though she already had The Cough, so how was she to know.

I'm very unhappy about it though, because I know my Dad and your Mum had planned for us to meet at your house very soon. Now that I might give you The Cough though, we'll have to wait for a while longer which is very sad. I'm sending you a picture of me being sad.

The other thing that makes me unhappy is that I missed out on a big thing yesterday. Rosie told me all about it through the wall. It's called The Feet or The Foot or something like that. I might have got that wrong as I couldn't hear very well and please bear in mind that this is my second language. Anyway, The Foot is when all the dogs that live around here get together in a big field nearby to run and play and sniff stuff and eat yummy food. They bring their people with them and the people put up little white flappy houses with flags on and things in them. (I actually saw them when Dad and I went for our walk but didn't go near them because of The Cough). There are sausages to eat and small people that are especially trained to drop bits of lovely food for you to find. One of the little flappy houses pours out big glasses of the scummy brown water that Dad likes. Rosie said she tried it and it was nice but too much of it would be bad for you.

There is also entertainment put on for you to bark at where people put bells on their legs and jump around waving bits of white cloth while someone else squeezes a box with something unhappy in it. At the end of the day there's a big competition where you show off your people and the dogs with the best people get prizes. I'm not sure how well I'd have done with my two, to be honest, but I love them anyway. It all sounds wonderful and I was very upset to miss it, but Rosie says it will happen again when the sun is in the same place in the sky so I'll be able to go then.

I asked Uncle Reefing about The Foot but he said he's never been. He says it sounds a bit like The Shoes he used to go to with Dad when he was younger and they used to jump things. He used to win things with Dad apparently and always came home with a ribbon. I think I'd like a ribbon so we'll have to practice a lot before the next Foot.

Mum found another of my marks the other day when she was giving me cuddles on the floor. It made her sad. This one is a patch on my neck under my chin where the skin is hard and no fur grows anymore. I don't really remember when I got it but I think it happened in the other place where I was tied up all the time. Sometimes I got tangled in the rope or if I got scared and tried to run away the rope would get tight and hurt me. I have a few marks like that - there's one on my face, one on my bottom and (although it's not very noticeable) a piece of my ear is missing. Mum and Dad get sad when they see them and Dad sometimes seems angry, but not at me. I have other marks too, but nobody can see those ones. A lot of dogs like me have them and if you're lucky you get to live with people who know you have these marks and accept you anyway and maybe even help the marks go away. I don't think you have marks, Milo. You and Rosie and Bertie are lucky that you've always lived with people who love you and take care of you. I'm still learning how to live like you do but it's hard to forget my marks. Sometimes a sound or a smell makes me think about something that happened in the other place and I get a little bit scared or anxious. Mum and Dad help me though and I know they will always look after me. Just like I'll always look after them.

I'm lying snuggled up next to Dad right now on the big bed with legs while I write to you, actually. He's looking at the square shiny thing in his hand (again!) but I think it will be time for bed soon because I'm falling asleep. HedgePig is already there but I need to find Hare and Phezzie first. Ducky still hasn't come back from rehab and I'm quite worried about him.

Goodnight Milo. Sleep well and I will write again soon.

Your good friend

Jackson

Good ropes and bad ropes – Hedges – Gracie goes away – Apollo's Story

4th July 2021

Dear Milo

I hope you are well.

I am very well, although because of The Cough it will still be a little while before I can meet up with you or other dogs and have a proper chat. I saw Rosie today but she was on the other side of the road and I wasn't allowed to talk to her which made me very upset. She was upset too which made me feel better.

We've been doing a lot of walking since I last wrote, and I've been thinking about it a bit. Do you remember in my last letter I told you about the rope that tied me up in the other place and how it hurt me? Well, I was thinking how strange it is that I still have ropes attached to me, but these ones are so different to how it used to be.

In the other place, I was tied up all the time and the rope hurt me and stopped me from going anywhere. The ropes here are the complete opposite. When I'm at home, I'm not tied up at all, and when the ropes are attached that means we're going out for an exciting adventure!

I have two ropes - we used to call them leads, and I think it's the same here - and I wear a different one depending on what we're going to do. When we're going out, Dad takes my clippy strappy thing off the hook and I always get excited when that happens. He holds it out and I stick my head straight through, which isn't as easy as it sounds when your bum won't stop wiggling. Once it's clipped up he puts on my short lead, which means we're going for a short walk.

The short lead means I have to stay close to Dad as he needs my help to cross the road and stay away from cars. We don't go on the road much, but when we do I always stop and look before crossing, unless I forget and Dad reminds me. Once we're off the road I can go a little further away but still stay pretty close, although sometimes I'd like to go further and faster but no matter how much I lean into it, Dad never speeds up. I used to lean a bit more when I first got here, I think, but it's usually more polite to let Dad set the pace. He's a bit old and can't run fast.

The best time is when he clips on the looooong lead! He says "sit" so I put my bottom on the ground and then wait for ages while he fusses around with tangles and clips and then attaches it to me. When he says "off you go" that means I can run off a long way before I have to stop. Sometimes I forget I have to stop and somehow spin around and end up facing where I've come from! I've noticed that Dad usually makes a "steaaady" noise just before it happens unless I slow down a bit so I'm still having a think about how all that works. He says other stuff too. "Come on" means I have to stop what I'm doing and follow him, and "Out" (usually in a loud Boss Man voice) means I have to come out of the special tall furry grass or I'll be in big trouble.

We had a great time today, while we were watching Uncle Reefing and his friend Wilf eating grass. I had my long lead on and could hardly feel it and barely knew it was there. I was running and jumping in the long grass while Dad walked behind me and then I noticed he wasn't holding the lead at all - it was on the ground behind me! He changed direction then and called me so I obviously stopped what I was doing and went straight over to him which made him very happy for some reason.

Ropes are funny things. When I wore one in the other place, it was horrible and it made me very unhappy. Over here though, the rope is a good thing. It means fun and excitement and it also tells me I'm safe because it means Mum and Dad are attached to me. Uncle Reefing wears one too, when he goes from his house to his field. He's so big and strong he could break the rope if he wanted or he could pull away and go wherever he liked.

He doesn't though, because he trusts Dad and knows that Dad will take care of him (as well as opening gates and stuff).

I'm looking forward to the time when I don't have to wear the long lead, of course, so I can run and jump and play and do whatever I want. I'll still be attached though. Like the marks I was telling you about, there are ropes you can see and some ropes you can't see. These are good things though. These ropes bring you home to your family, even though you don't have to go. They make you look after your people. They make your people look after you and search for you if you're lost and give you cuddles and take you for walks and tell you you're a good boy even when you think you're not. These ropes have two ends and are the strongest ropes in the world.

Do you have hedges where you are, Milo? I love hedges. We didn't have many in the other place so now I make sure I check them out whenever I can. There's lots of good things in the hedges around here but you have to get right into them to investigate properly. You should always leave your tail out so your people know where you are, however. I'll show you my favourites when you come to visit. I've attached a picture of me looking for birds in one.

The rain has started again so I think I'll go to bed now. Phezzie is unwell and HedgePig is quite stinky too. Ducky hasn't come back yet. Hare is fine though.

Goodnight Milo. Keep being a good boy.

Your friend

Jackson

11th July 2021

Dear Milo

I hope you and your people are well.

We have had some sad news here. Do you remember a while ago Mum and Dad and I went on a long trip to see an old lady named Gracie? Gracie was very old and very tired and the other day she decided she had to go away. Her Mum and Dad were there when she left and they were very sad. Gracie lived with them since she was very little and they all loved each other very much. My Mum and Dad used to look after her every now and then when she lived nearby and I'll never forget how happy she was to see them the last time we met, once she realised who they were. I'm very glad I got to meet her before she left. She was a very, very good dog.

Meeting Gracie made me think a little bit about growing old. I think sometimes when people bring a dog into their family they don't always think about what it will be like when they grow old, especially when it's a little puppy. Being the dog of a family is a big responsibility. We have to look after our people and do everything we can to keep them safe. If we are lucky and we find the right people, they will love us and do everything they have to in order to take care of us too, like Gracie's Mum and Dad did for her. I think being old must be hard if you don't have people to help you. I remember that Gracie couldn't run fast and couldn't see or hear very well (and thought I was her nephew) but she was very happy because she was loved. And she was loved right up to the time she went away. Her Mum and Dad didn't want her to go but they knew she had to, so gave her the help she needed, even though it made them very sad. I think Gracie was very lucky.

I remember when I lived in the other place, after the Lovely Lady helped me and before I came to live here, I lived with a lot of other dogs. It was a very nice place and we had a lot of fun running and playing together, but it wasn't really home and we weren't a family. I was only there a little while but there were some dogs that were there a long time. A lot of these dogs were old and it must have been hard for them to see puppies and young dogs like me come in and go to our new homes while they were left behind again. I wonder about these dogs sometimes. I think how sad it is that some of them will go away without ever knowing what it's like to lie on the big bed on legs with their Dad cuddling them, just like I'm doing right now. My life was hard, but things can change completely if you can find the family you fit into. I think that although they don't know it, some families need an old dog that is just looking to be loved until they have to go away. It's very hard, but sometimes important things are the hardest to do.

I spoke to a dog a long way away the other day. Mum was talking to a little man on her people box and I heard a dog shouting so I shouted back. Apparently, I was talking to a little dog in a place called America. That's where Uncle Reefing's grandfather came from but the little dog didn't know him. He was very nice.

We had a visitor yesterday and I liked her very much. I usually take my time with new people and make sure they're nice before I talk to them but all the people I've met here have been nice so I decided very quickly that I liked her. I liked her so much that I climbed into her lap while she was sitting outside. Well, half-into her lap anyway as she was quite small and I'm a big dog. I haven't done that to anyone else apart from Mum and Dad before. Maybe Rosie is right when she says everybody is her friend.

I forgot! I don't have The Cough anymore! I got to play with Rosie today for the first time in ages and it was lovely. We ran around the place with the grass and the big hedge behind my house and had a great time. I missed Rosie and I hope you like her when you meet her. She's lovely.

All of my friends and back and in great form, HedgePig especially. He was gone for ages but has put on a lot of weight and is now quite chubby. He still squeaks when I chew his bottom though.

There seems to be a lot of shouting outside because of some men who were chasing a ball earlier so I must go and bark at them now. Sleep well and do an extra spin for me before you lie down.

Your good friend

Jackson

18th July 2021

Dear Milo

Well this is more like it! Finally the sun is out and it feels lovely and warm like where I came from. Of course, Mum and Dad don't seem to know how to deal with it at all. Everyone knows that when it's hot you stay where it's cool, drink lots of water and don't move much. They insist on going outside in the middle of the day and digging things in the grass or moving things around and then come back inside all hot and smelly, wondering why they're tired. I'm trying to train them up and so far they understand enough that we only go out for walks very early or very late when the air is cool. When Uncle Reefing is too hot he just stands at his gate and shouts until somebody brings him inside. It's slow going, but I think they're getting it. My day is spent either snoozing in the coolest part of the house or sitting in my pool. It's not too bad here, really.

May I ask you a personal question? It's a bit embarrassing, but something that I've wondered about since I go here.

Do your people collect your poo?

In the other place, poo just happened and it eventually disappeared. When I did the first one here though, on the night I arrived, it was like I'd given Mum and Dad the best present ever. I got treats and cuddles and was told I was the best boy ever. And then things got even stranger. Mum put this little bag over her front paw and PICKED IT UP! Ever since then, they've picked up every single one, wherever and whenever I've produced it. I found it all very embarrassing and wouldn't have mentioned it until the other day, while we were on our walk, we met a very nice Staffie named Beau and her Mum who lives near us. As soon as Dad saw them he waved our bag of poo at them and then Beau's Mum waved one back! Hers was much smaller than mine though. I chatted with Beau (who was as embarrassed as I was) and apparently her Mum collects poo too, as do a lot of the people around here. Not everyone does it though. We sometimes come across leavings while we're out and about and Dad shakes his head and makes tutting noises when he sees it. It appears that over here, if you want to be a good dog person, you should make sure you don't leave your dog's poo behind and take it home with you. I understand why too. Pee-mails are important and tell you lots of stuff, but all poo does is make things smelly and make you poorly if you get too close or even accidentally eat it a couple of times. It's definitely best for everyone if it's taken away and put somewhere else.

I think something like that happened to me today. When we were out this morning I found something that looked yummy and while Dad wasn't looking I scoffed it down really quickly and there was nothing left for him to see. Later on though Rosie came to visit and I was feeling very quiet and poorly and didn't want to play at all, even though she came into the house and took Phezzie into the garden without asking. After a while I had a small unpleasantness and felt much better afterwards. Even though it's late I wanted to jump around and play and Dad used some of his special words again.

Something happened with Bertie the other day that wasn't nice. We were walking and met Bertie and Rosie. I knew Bertie was in a funny mood and didn't want to go talk to them but I couldn't make Dad understand. When we got close, Bertie growled and jumped on me and shouted to stay away from Rosie. I got a terrible scare and yelped and whined, even though he didn't actually hurt me. Milo, he got SUCH a telling off from his Dad. I hid behind my Dad and Bertie's mum came straight over and made a big fuss of me and gave me loads of sausage, which I ate even though I was scared. I was sad that Bertie was angry with me, but I think he was worried that I might try to take Rosie away. I think when I meet him again we will try to make up but I'll be extra careful. I think Dad will listen to me next time too. Rosie told me not to worry and that she's still my friend and that

Bertie doesn't own her and she doesn't need his permission to do anything.

I was thinking about the other place earlier and I realised I've never told you about Apollo. He's a very important dog where I come from, and he has helped lots and lots of dogs like me. It's a bit late now and I'm tired from sleeping all day, but I'll tell you all about him very soon. He's a real hero to all of us and it's very important that we tell his story.

Goodnight Milo. Look after your people and stay safe.

Your friend

Jackson

25th July 2021

Dear Milo

Hello! I hope you are doing well! It has been very hot since I last wrote so I hope you have been managing to stay cool. I have been in and out of my pool every day and we often go to the river near here for a swim.

Rosie tells me that over here everybody always talks about the weather so I've been practising so I can fit in. I hope I'm doing it properly.

We had a big adventure today and went somewhere I've never been before. We got in the car and I thought we were going to The Yard but we didn't. Instead we went to a place near here that was very strange. When the car stopped and Dad opened the door I was in a big space with lots and lots of other cars all standing still except for some that were moving very slowly. I had a good sniff around and was very excited by all the smells and sounds. Then we went to a gap in a big wall that had glass in it and when we got close the glass moved aside all on its own! That was quite scary but Mum and Dad went through so I did as well. Inside the big wall was a bit like the grassy place next to home where I play, but it was much

much bigger with lots and lots of the flowery growing things that Mum sticks in the ground. Except these weren't in the ground. These were all in big bowls and there were lots of the same ones all standing together on the ground and on big tables. In between the tables there were people with shiny squeaky rattly things on wheels and every now and then one of the people would take a flowery thing and put it on the rattly thing.

When I looked around Mum had one of the rattly things too and was looking very closely at all the flowery things while Dad and I waited patiently. I think I was better at waiting than Dad though because he kept shuffling his feet and looking at the ticky thing he carries on his arm.

When Mum was finished and the rattly thing was full we went into a huge big house and Milo, I have never seen anything like it. It was full of shiny things and smelly things and paper things and chairs and big beds on legs and swingy things. It was amazing, and a bit scary to be honest. There were lots of people around so I made sure to stick close to Dad to look after him. At the end we left Mum standing in a line with lots of other people and went through another door where there were more toys than I have ever seen in my whole life! I think Dad wanted me to pick one but it was all a bit too much and I didn't want to stay so we went outside where everyone was very happy with me a gave me cuddles and told me what a Good Boy I was - even people I didn't know! It was all very strange and odd but I liked it and hope to go back again some day.

I met Bertie again today, and we have made up and are friends again. Rosie wasn't with us so he was happy to sniff, although I'm still a bit nervous. He's very big and strong so I think I'll stay being careful for a while longer. It was nice to see him as his usual friendly bouncy self though. And his mum gave me more sausage which was nice.

I mentioned Apollo in my last letter so I think it's time to tell you his story. Or part of it anyway, as it's very long and important.

Apollo was born a very long time ago, in a warm dry place like the one I came from. Like me he was very loved by his mummy when he was a pup and she kept him warm and made sure he had a full tummy. But, again like me, when he was very little a man came and took him away. Apollo had his people and he knew his job from the very beginning. He had to love his people and look after them and find birds for them and in return they were supposed to love him and take care of him too.

But they didn't.

Apollo was a Very Good Boy and did his very best to do his job and make The Man happy. Sometimes he got things wrong though, like I do. He didn't understand what The Man wanted him to do or he wanted to play instead of work or he ate something he wasn't supposed to because he was hungry. He lived outside and was often cold and hungry and sometimes The Man did bad things to him even though he was doing his best.

One day The Man decided he didn't want Apollo to live with them anymore. Instead of finding him a new home with people who did want him though, The Man did a terrible thing. He hurt Apollo's eyes very badly and then took him to a place nobody goes and tied him to a tree.

And then he left.

I don't know why he did what he did. I don't think anyone does. We know people can be mean sometimes but this was a terrible, terrible thing.

Apollo was very scared. He wasn't able to see anything anymore but he could smell and hear everything around him but couldn't go anywhere because of the chain around his neck. He was also very brave and very strong and he knew he wasn't ready to go away, even though The Man had left him no food and no water. Apollo fought and fought to stay until, one morning a long time after The Man had left him, he smelled something wonderful and heard a gentle voice. A Lady had found him.

The Lady was very sad at first and cried and cried when she saw what The Man had done. She knew that although you have to cry sometimes, it doesn't really do very much to help, so she stopped and wiped her eyes. Then she gently stroked Apollo's head and undid the chain tying him to the tree.

The dog who told me Apollo's story says the Lady who found him was an Angel. I don't know what that is but Uncle Reefing says there are different kinds of people. Some people, like The Man who hurt Apollo are mean and bad. Most people are good and won't hurt you and would cry if they had found Apollo like he was. Then there are people who do things. Like the Lady who helped Apollo. She was sad and cried but then she took the next step and did something to help him. There aren't a lot of those people and I think that's what Angels are.

I think that's enough for now as I'm running out of room but I'll tell you more in my next letter. Please don't worry though. This is a sad story but it has a wonderful ending.

Be a good boy, Milo. I'll write again soon.

Your friend

Jackson

*A bit of a wander – Apollo's Angels – A new
view of Uncle Reefing*

1ˢᵗ August 2021

Dear Milo

How are you? I hope you are well. I'm very well and
happy.

Since I last wrote, I'm glad to say that all my friends have
come back and are in fine order. Phezzie has had some
work done and although his beak is now much shorter
and looks quite odd it's lovely to see him again. Ducky
has far fewer holes in him and smells much better. Hare
and HedgePig are as well as ever, though Hare has
become a little floppy recently.

Something happened the other day that felt wonderful at
the time but when I think about it, I'm afraid I might
have done something bad. Mum's people box wasn't
working and a man came to fix it by doing some stuff to
the things that stick out of the walls at home. I kept a
close eye on him and made sure he didn't get too close
while he was inside and while he was in the grassy bit at

the back. He was nice though and gave me a pat even though I was trying to be a bit fierce.

When he was gone I checked things out to see if he had done everything properly and I noticed that I could see a little bit of outside through the big door in the wall around the grassy bit. I gave it a little bump with my nose and then I could see even more outside so I popped my head out for a look. I still couldn't see very much so I leaned forward and then my front feet were outside and then suddenly entirely by accident all of me was outside. I wasn't quite sure what to do next so I went to where Rosie lives to see if she could tell me but she wasn't home. Then I thought I'd save Dad a job and take myself for a walk, so off I went!

I decided that I'd stick to the places I know so followed the trail that Dad and I normally follow when we go for a long walk. I went up the track to where it crosses the ditch by the big field of furry grass and then followed the muddy water the whole way as far as the big tree. It was wonderful. I didn't have anything trailing behind me and I could run as far and as fast as I wanted without getting tangled up and without having to stop suddenly. I could follow birds and stop and have a proper sniff without having to Leave It. Normally, when we get to the big tree I have to stop and let Dad go first. As I was on my own I didn't really know what to do so decided I'd just turn around and go home and that's what I did.

As I turned around, out of the corner of my eye I saw a little light and heard a little beep from my collar but didn't pay too much attention to it. I just followed the path back the way I came until I got back to where it crosses the muddy water.

Now, there is a place here where I've never been allowed to go and it has always smelled very exciting. There isn't really a path and it's very close to the furry grass but I suddenly smelled a bird really close so I went to investigate. I stuck my nose to the ground and ran back and forth and back and forth looking for that silver thread of scent and then I found it! So I followed. And followed and followed and followed, into the bushes and across the open and through the furry grass. You know what it's like when you're on the scent - I was there for ages and ages or it might have only been a very short time.

And then I heard something very strange - I heard HedgePig! Now, as you know HedgePig isn't allowed out of the house so how could I hear him all the way out here?!? I lifted my head up out of the furry grass but I couldn't see anything so instead I kept listening for HedgePig's squeak and headed towards it until my head popped out of the grass and there was Mum and HedgePig! I was a bit worried I'd be in trouble but went straight to Mum when she called me and I don't think I've ever seen her so happy. She gave me a great big cuddle and told me I was a Very Good Boy. She did hold onto my collar as soon as I got to her mind you, and didn't let go.

Then she talked into the little square thing she and Dad carries and next thing I see is Dad running across the field toward us, looking very hot and puffy. He was on the other side of the muddy water so I thought we'd hear the special words again but instead he went a different way and very soon he was with us too. He also gave me a great big cuddle too and told me I was a Very Good Boy. Then we went to the car which was parked in a very odd place and went home. I had a lovely time.

When I told Uncle Reefing what had happened he was very upset. He said the world is not a safe place for dogs like me and I should never go out on my own. There are bad people out there who will take dogs away from their families and send them to places where they're not looked after properly, or even worse. He says that what I did made Mum and Dad very worried and very unhappy, even though the little box on my collar told them exactly where I was all the time they were looking for me.

I don't want to make Mum and Dad unhappy, and I don't want to be stolen away from my home and go back to the place I came from. I'm not ever going to go outside on my own again and will only go when Mum or Dad are with me and I will listen to them and always come back straight away when they call me. Unless I forget, of course, which might happen. In any case there's a there's a bright new clicky thing on the big door to outside now so I don't think there's much chance of me going anywhere without them anyway.

Do you have cats where you are, Milo? There is one cat I meet most days on my walks. I say cat, but I think he's a tiger because he's very huge and very fierce. Last time I saw him, I was just trying to be friendly and see if he wanted to play when suddenly he grew twice as big and made very scary hissy spitty noises at me even though I wasn't even near him. To protect Mum, I let out a big yelp and ran away behind her up a grassy bank. She didn't seem to understand though and made a kind of tutting noise at me before saying nice words to the cat! Yes! To the actual cat! Sometimes I think people are very hard to understand.

I started to tell you Apollo's story when I last wrote and I think I got to where the Angel saw what The Man had done to poor Apollo's eyes and decided she had to help him.

Apollo was still frightened when the Angel found him because even though he's always done his best the people he had known were cruel and hurt him. He started to realise the Angel was different though. Her voice was soft and her hands oh so gentle as she undid the chain around his neck, stroked his head and gave him a big drink of lovely cool water. He had been tied there for days, remember, with nothing to eat or drink. Although Apollo was strong inside, his body was very weak so the Angel had to carry him home even though he was big and she was small. I think she was very strong inside too.

When she got him home she and the other angels she knew set to, helping Apollo, healing his wounds and making him better. Have you ever had a grass seed in your ear or your paw, Milo? If you have you know how much it can hurt. Now imagine how terrible it would be to have one in your eye. Well, Apollo had more grass seeds in his eyes than you or I could count, Milo. But he didn't complain. People had only ever been cruel to him, but he trusted the Angels and let them help him because he knew that they loved him, even though he'd just met them.

Apollo needed a LOT of help. That much help is hard to find so just like someone showed my picture to Mum and Dad, one of the Angels showed Apollo's picture to another Angel who lives over here and she decided to help him too. She showed his picture to lots and lots of other people who live with Pointer dogs like me and they all wanted to help too. She collected up all the help that people gave and passed it on to Apollo's Angels who worked really long and hard to take his pain away and make him better. In fact all the wonderful people gave so much help that Apollo didn't need it all and his

Angels decided to use it the rest of it for other Pointers over there that were sad and poorly and unloved.

In the end, although Apollo would never be able to see again, he was well and happy and then another amazing thing happened. One of the Angels had so much love to give that they said they would like Apollo to come over here and live with them forever, just like what happened with me coming to live with Mum and Dad. So that's what happened. He went up in the air and travelled over here, but the help still kept coming and Apollo's Angels kept finding more and more dogs that needed their help.

Next time I'll tell you more about what happened to Apollo when he got here, but his story is about more than him now. It's about him and me and Luna and Chester and Indra and Silver and Mara and all the other dogs he has helped. And we'll never forget him.

Goodnight Milo. Sleep well and be happy.

Your good friend

Jackson

8th August 2021

Dear Milo

I hope you and your people are well and you're looking after them.

As you know I've been very busy looking after Dad recently as he's been a bit sad and I think I'm making him feel better. I did something by accident the other day that made him very happy. At least I think it made him happy because although he blew his nose and wiped his eyes he gave me the biggest cuddles. We were in the place behind the house where he was doing something to the prickly hedge and was wearing sock things (gloveses I think they're called) on his front paws. When the time came to go inside I picked up the gloveses and brought them with me and when Dad saw he was very excited and called Mum outside to see. Apparently, according to Uncle Reefing, Grandad Pollock used to help Dad's granny like this. Every morning she would walk to a big house with a bell on it and every morning Grandad Pollock went with her. He'd then wait outside while she did whatever it was she was doing and then he'd walk her home again, but used to help by carrying her gloveses for her. And I did the same!

I've been a very good boy and have been working on waiting and sitting and coming back to Mum and Dad when they call. I'm getting better at listening to them and remembering what to do but sometimes it's really hard. For a while I couldn't tell if I was getting better or not, and even thought I might be getting worse! I would forget a lot or get distracted by birds and disappear into a hedge when I'm supposed to be listening, and sometimes I couldn't hear Mum or Dad even though they were right beside me. Uncle Reefing told me this is how learning works and I need to be patient but it's hard and I worried that I was doing things wrong or I wasn't good enough. Reefing said not to worry and that we all learn together and one day it will feel like it's what I've done all my life and I won't even have to think about it.

And you know what? I think he might be right. He usually is.

Today we went for a run in the big field with the long grass where he and Wilf spend their days, and Dad didn't hold onto the big long line at all. I ran all over the place and even though there were really interesting smells I ran over to him every time he called me and waited when he asked me to and when I found Mum lying down in the long grass I lay down beside her and waited for Dad to reach us. They seemed very happy with me.

Do you look at your paws much, Milo? Mum found a little thing on one of mine that she thought was a tick at first, but it wasn't. It looks like one though. At least I think it does as I can't see it very well. We ended up going for a drive in the car to see the V.E.T. again as she wanted to make sure it was nothing nasty. It doesn't hurt and I don't pay any attention to it so I think it's just a warty thing that will probably fall off on its own. The V.E.T. is an old friend of Mum and Dad's and she was very kind and gentle. It was nice to meet her but I don't really need to see her again for a while. I'll keep a close eye on the warty thing just to make sure. I have a picture of it - what do you think? Have you ever seen anything like that before?

We had some visitors the other evening and one of them was a very small squawky person that made a lot of noise. I tried to beat him at noisemaking but he won as I got told off. I thought that was unfair as I was in my own house but I suppose you have to be polite to guests. They all sat outside making food on the outdoor hot burny thing but I stayed inside until they quieted down a bit. When I did come out, the people were quiet and waited for me to talk to them, which was nice. There's nothing more uncomfortable than having a stranger rush up to you and put their paws all over you and act like they're your best friend when they've never met you before. I'll always be polite when that happens but I prefer it when people give me room. One man was particularly nice and I climbed up on him so he'd give me some cheese. That was great and I could see Dad was happy with me too.

I need to finish telling you Apollo's story. The Angels had helped him and he was feeling much better. A wonderful lady over here wanted him to come and live with her and that's what happened. Apollo was very happy but then a very sad thing happened and his new people had to go away. Apollo missed his people, but his Angels looked after him even though they'd gone away. They had arranged that he would go to live with the Lovely Lady - the Angel - who first saw his picture and helped him and lots of other dogs like him. Apollo is the dog that we all want to be - the easiest, kindest dog you could ever hope to meet. He lived with his Angel for a long, long time and all the while he worked with her and lots of other people to help dogs in the other place that were hurt or hungry and needed good people. Lots and lots and lots of dogs. More dogs than you or I could count and he did this for longer than you or I could remember.

Then one day came when he was very old and he had to go away. But he was a Very Good Boy - the Best Boy - and he was ready even though his Mum was very sad to say goodbye. Even though terrible things had been done to him by cruel people he always had love in his heart for the people around him and they all loved him too. He had a long life, filled with amazing things and the most wonderful thing of all is that even though he's gone away, he's still doing his job, taking care of dogs that need his help.

Dogs just like me.

Without Apollo and his Angels I wouldn't be here, so I will never forget him or be able to thank them enough. The best thing I can do is try to copy him and help the dogs that are still in the other place, even if it's just by telling his story.

Goodnight Milo. Keep your nose wet.

Your good friend

Jackson

15th August 2021

Dear Milo

I hope you and your people are well. I am very well thank you very much. My warty thing hasn't changed and doesn't bother me at all so that's good.

It's been an interesting time since I last wrote and although home and Mum and Dad are the same there have been some very big changes all around us. The furry grass has all gone and there's just this prickly proggly stuff left behind. When we were walking in the field the other day there was a big car with a huge spinny thing on the front that was eating the top of the furry grass. That was followed later by another big car that ate up what was left behind and put out either a big poo or a bit square egg - I'm not sure which. Either way, those corners must hurt! They were all collected together into a huge pile bigger than our house and then taken away.

It's all a little bit sad really as the birds that used to live in the furry grass have all gone somewhere else and these big mean grey and white birds with hooked beaks that smell of water and salt have come instead. They're a bit scary to be honest and I don't like them very much. I don't snorfle around as much as I used to but I'm sure the nice birds will come back really soon.

While all this was going on we met a man who was sitting in his car watching it all happen and Dad stopped to talk to him for a while. He was a nice man who very gently tugged at my ears while he was talking. He was hot and dusty and seemed very tired. He smelled of the earth and of the grass and the sun and of the rain. Underneath that he smelled of work and of worry. But above everything and underneath everything he smelled of hope. Hope for a future where things grow and thrive and life wins through. Have you ever met someone, Milo, who seems to be exactly where they're supposed to be? That's what this man was like. He is part of the land, helping it and all of us with new life and new hope. He is a good man and I and the other dogs around here are very lucky that we're able to explore the land he loves and cares for.

I told Uncle Reefing about the proggly field and he was very happy to hear it. He said it means he and Dad can go for a proper run. I'm not sure what he's excited about to be honest. I've seen Dad run and it usually ends up with him leaning on his knees and wheezing after a few metres. Sometimes I wonder if I should believe everything Uncle Reefing tells me.

Having said that, I've noticed that more and more Mum and Dad don't bother holding onto my long lead when we're out and about. I still love to follow and follow when I smell birds but I seem to hear Mum and Dad a bit more when they call me now. One day when I was a long way away, Dad called me so I lifted my head, looked back and ran over to see what he wanted. As it turned out he just wanted to give me some cheese so that was great. He was very happy to see me and I got lots of cuddles and was told I was a Very Good Boy too. I still love to find and follow birds but I'm beginning to think now that sometimes there might be something nicer to do.

We have new neighbours! I've met them and they seem very nice although they don't smell of dog yet. We will have a long time to get to know each other and I'm a bit excited that they have a big garden that doesn't have a dog in it so I'll have to explore it soon and make sure it's all safe and secure. I've started by checking the wall around the front bit and it seems fine.

Do you remember I went to a place a little while ago with big walls and a slidy door and lots of flowery growing things that inside? Well, we went back there again and I was very brave this time. We went to the place where all the toys were and I picked out a new friend! Actually, to be fair I picked one out but when Dad flipped over the papery bit he went a bit pale and quickly put it back so I ended up taking Monkey home instead. I carried him to the big line of people, which everybody seemed to think was nice, and then after waiting a little bit brought him back to the car so we could go home. Monkey is great and has a big squeaky nose but to be honest he's no Hare. Hare has gone away for a little rest and I'm sure she'll come back soon.

Rosie has been on holiday somewhere else and says she had a very nice time. It's funny to think that when I first got here I thought I was on holiday and would go back to the hot dry place I came from. I don't know why anyone would want to go on holiday from here where you have everything you could want. Rosie says that sometimes it's nice to see and smell something different but I'm not sure. I don't know if we're planning to go on holiday but if we do I hope it's just like home.

I liked the picture I saw of you, Milo, running through the big tall green stuff. Please be careful though! I would be very worried if I was out like that and couldn't see Mum or Dad. I think that sometimes for dogs like me it's hard to understand that your people are there for you, even if you can't see them. Some of us have been left on our own for so long that we are very frightened of being alone and cry when our people leave us because we think they're never going to come back. If you're lucky, like you and me, they always do, so we don't need to worry.

Stay well, Milo. Always go back to your Mum when she calls you.

Your friend

Jackson

22nd August 2021

Dear Milo

Is this what it's like here all the time? I had just gotten used to being nice and warm and now it's rainy and wet again! I don't know if I'll ever get used to this. I hope you are well, by the way.

I've been doing some work with my people recently. They can be a bit slow when we're walking and sometimes it's almost like they've completely stopped! When that happens I stop so they can catch up and then when the lead goes loose I move on again. I'm beginning to think that maybe I should just slow down a little so the lead is slack all the time and they can keep up. I've also been practising "With Me". That's what Mum says that when she's a bit scared and wants me to stay beside her to look after her. I'm very good at this one. One day after our walk I felt I had been so good I deserved some of the fizzy water she and Dad were drinking but I wasn't allowed which was very unfair. Instead I went and had a drink from the bird bath which is totally fine.

Do you remember last time when I said I wasn't sure whether I should believe everything Uncle Reefing tells me? Well, I take that back. He talked about going for a run with Dad and I got completely the wrong idea and will never not believe him again.

Today, as it was nice and dry and sunny Mum took me to The Yard. Dad was already there as Reefing needed him to tidy up his house and make his bed. When we got to The Yard though, Mum didn't put on my long lead and we didn't go the usual way. Instead we went up another track to a gate that led into a huge big field full of the proggly grass that Reefing likes. Mum didn't go in but just leaned on the gate instead and looked around. I poked my head through so I could have a look too and could see something moving, a long way away. It was going really really fast and as it got closer I heard a sound like you hear in the sky before there's a big light and the rain starts to fall. Then I realised it was Uncle Reefing and Dad was on his back! Literally sitting on him! I felt the ground shake under my paws and then they flashed past us almost too fast to see.

Milo, I never imagined I'd see Uncle Reefing like this. He's usually plodding around his field or dozing in his house, but now he was going faster than anything I've ever seen, and his face, Milo! His ears were pricked forward and he looked fierce and proud and focused and happy and determined and really quite scary. Mum kept her hand on my head all the time though so I knew everything was ok. And there was more! After they'd gone past us there was what looked like a bit of a wooden wall, standing up on its own, taller than I am. I was sure they were going to stop but they didn't. It was like they grew invisible wings because they just flew right over the top of it like the biggest bird I've ever seen.

After a little while they came back and Uncle Reefing was so happy he was bouncing and jogging and mainly going sideways. Dad was very happy too, giving him big pats and telling him how good he is. After he had a shower and a brush off (neither of which I like) we brought him and Wilf to their field so they could have a roll and eat grass. Reefing says he's still got it, although he'll pay for it tomorrow. I think he means he'll feel a bit stiff, but that's ok. He's quite old and that's allowed. Luckily he says Dad gives him some medicine every day that makes him feel better and allows him to have fun. I think that I'll keep taking the medicine Mum and Dad give me, even if sometimes it's a bit yucky.

Seeing Uncle Reefing like that makes me think about the older ones around me and wonder what they were like when they were young. Because they were all young once and did great things. When he was my age, Reefing and Dad went around jumping huge big jumps (not shoes) and winning ribbons and prizes. His friend Wilf was able to run really, really fast - faster than Reefing even - and lots of times was the fastest horse out of all the horses around him. They have another friend at The Yard named Razz and he and his Mum were really, really, really good at dancing. He was better than other horses from this place and lots of other places too. Now he's quite hairy and stands in his field enjoying the sun on his back, and although he doesn't dance anymore he still loves his Mum and she loves him.

I think it's easy to forget that the old ones are just the same as us, except a bit further along the road. I remember some of the old dogs I knew in the other place and the stories they had and someday, a long time from now, I want to be just like them and like Uncle Reefing.

Are you allowed to help when your Mum digs, Milo? I'm not. I've made some holes in the grass but I don't think my people appreciate my work because when I go back they've been filled in again and things put over them. Sometimes I think they just don't appreciate me and wonder how they'd feel if I stopped helping altogether. We all know I'm just going to keep on doing my bit though.

I think I might like a different place to sleep these days so have been trying out a few others to see what they're like. It means I have to drag my blanket back and forth through the entire house of course but I think it's worth the effort. Tonight I'm going to try the room where Mum talks to people on her little people box. I had a chat with a dog who lives in a place called France a little while ago. She was very nice but talked a lot about going to the toilet.

Rosie is very well. I visited her in her house the other day. Since Bertie jumped on me I've been a bit worried about meeting other dogs - even Rosie - but I suddenly remembered how lovely it is to run and jump about and wrestle and before I knew it I was back to my old self. We even had a game of running up and down on either side of the fence this evening, which was lovely.

I must go, Milo, as I need to decide who will keep me company tonight. Ducky and Hare are away for a rest, so I think it will have to be Phezzie and HedgePig. Monkey is in disgrace as he has blotted his copybook. I will tell you about that next time.

Goodnight Milo. Keep wagging that tail.

Your friend

Jackson

Holidays oop North – More friends and family – Home again

5th September 2021

Dear Milo

I'm on holiday! Imagine that!

A few days ago I got a bit worried because Mum rolled up my bed and shoved it into the back of the car with loads and loads of other stuff. I thought she and Dad were going to go away and leave me but they put on my clippy strappy thing and put me into the back of the car too, on my very smart new rug, and we set off on a really long trip. I was very comfy though and stayed asleep for most of it. Hare and Ducky kept me company. After a long time we stopped at a place like the one where I first met Mum and Dad but there were a lot more people at this one and lots and lots of cars. I had a wee and a drink and then we went and sat down by a big building so people could see what a good and handsome boy I am. I know that because they all said so.

We got back into the car then and drove for a long time again until we stopped at a nice house on the side of a big hill. I didn't know the people who live there but Mum and Dad did and we were very welcome and all got big hugs. I felt a bit shy at first but then saw the people were very nice so had a lovely time looking around. I met some Collie dogs who talked funny - they said "eh up" instead of hello and said I was a "reet grand lad". They seemed very nice. I also got to see where Mum and Dad sleep so for the first time ever I slept in their bed instead of my own! They were a bit surprised when I jumped up but Dad put soft squishy things in his ears before going to sleep and seemed very glad to have them. I slept very well and didn't move until it was time to get up.

The next day we got back in the car and went driving again but I brought a new friend with me. He looks a bit like Uncle Reefing but has long ears and is grey and his name is t'Donkeh. The nice people we stayed with gave him to me and I love him very much. After another long drive we came to a little house next to a big house with the scummy brown water that Dad likes and Mum brought all my stuff into the little house. It was another new place so I didn't really like it at first but now it's fine. After I had my dinner we went to the big house so Mum and Dad could eat and I was a very good boy and sat quietly by their table all the time. Lots of people stopped to talk to me and Dad kept stroking me to make sure I wasn't worried but I was happy to give everyone a sniff. That night I wanted to climb up onto Mum and Dad's bed again but apparently I'm only allowed on my own bed here which is sad.

The next day, after a walk and breakfast we got in the car again and drove a little way for me to meet my Granny! She's even littler than Mum and I was very careful to be gentle around her in case I accidentally knocked her over. She sounds like Mum too. She has very nice cheese though and keeps giving me some even when Mum and Dad have stopped. The only thing that bothered me was that a cat lives in her house but I didn't meet her so that's OK.

We went for a big long walk today through some woods and up a great big hill into some fields with prickly bushes and lots of bunnies. Dad fell over and used his special words again but that was definitely not my fault. On the way back down a wonderful thing happened - we met some English Pointers! Their names were Ripley and Harris and they were very nice and friendly. Ripley is older than me and Harris is younger but they are both a LOT bigger! I thought they sounder funny - telling me I'm "oop north", saying things like "why-aye, man" and talking a lot about "canny bags" of something nice. They thought I sounded funny though, so I think we're all the same really. We just sound different; not wrong or bad, just different.

I think we'll watch the people-box again tonight. I'm getting used to it now and just snooze while I listen to the voices and it's nice. I might keep doing it when we get home. It's funny, but when I first came to Mum and Dad I thought I was on holiday, but I didn't really know what a holiday was then. The most important thing about holidays is going home and now that I have a real home and I know I'll go back there, my holidays are even better.

I must go now. Dad and I are sitting in front of our little house and there are some dogs in the grassy bit in front of the big house next door that I really have to talk to. I know we're near the sea here and I'd really like to see it again. Maybe they can tell me.

Goodnight Milo. Don't knock anyone over, even if it's by accident.

Your good friend

Jackson

12th September 2021

Dear Milo

Home again! Our holiday "oop north" was lovely but it's nice to be home again smelling all the smells and seeing the places that I know. I have so much to tell you I don't think I can fit it in one letter but I'll put in all I can for now.

Have you ever been to the beach, Milo? I have and it was wonderful. I didn't quite know what to make of the soft sand when we got there but as soon as Dad put on my long lead I was off like a shot. Sand is funny stuff. Sometimes it's really soft so running is hard but other times it's hard and you can run really really fast. It seems to be hardest near the sea but that's where the splashy crashy wet happens and that can be a bit scary when it's really big. There was also loads of this brown stuff that kind of looks like planty things but tastes really salty and flops around when you pick it up. I didn't like it but kept trying in case it changed.

There was one bit near some big rocks where the splashy crashy wet wasn't very big so I went for a paddle in the water which I really liked. Then I went out on one of the rocks and then suddenly what I thought was rock wasn't rock and I was properly swimming! I'm a good swimmer but that was a bit of a surprise so I went straight back to Dad to make sure he was ok. I was a very good listener all through my holiday and went back to Mum and Dad whenever they called and they looked very proud of me. I'm sending you a picture of me on the beach with a very big old house behind me made out of stones. There were a lot of big old houses on our holidays but some of them were very broken.

We went to the beach every day and I loved it so much that I brought quite a bit of it back with me and put it in the back of Dad's car. There were a lot of people and dogs on the beach though so I didn't always get to run as far and as fast as I wanted, but it was nice to meet them. It's funny how you know even before they say anything that some people really like dogs and some people don't. People we don't even know stopped to speak to us and they always looked at me while they were there so I think they were talking about me. I tried to be as friendly as I could and you know what - I'm getting better at it and it's much easier now! I played with so many dogs, too - Labradors and spaniels and terriers and all sorts. It was great.

One night I met Grandad. He's Mum's Dad. He's very tall and I liked him straight away even though his pats are quite...vigorous. I was very happy in his house and pottered around after him which made Mum and Dad happy too. Grandad has a lot of food in his house but doesn't have a dog or a cat to keep him company. Grandad talks funny. Like Mum when she's excited except more so. I'm not sure Dad can understand either of them, to be honest. I know I don't!

Another day we went to visit other friends in a place with lots and lots of houses. I must be getting used to going to different places now because I trotted straight into their house and then was very good and wandered around their grassy place without digging stuff up or going into the planty things or breaking anything. I got some yummy treats for being a Good Boy and not being A Disgrace.

The house where we stayed was very nice and had a grassy place in front where I could sit and watch everybody go by as well as talk to dogs in the grassy place of the big house next door. Lots of different dogs visited there and waited while their people ate or drank the scummy brown water so it was nice to have a sniff across the fence with them and they all made me very welcome. People stopped to talk to us all the time and by the time we left the small people would all wave and say my name when they passed our gate and the big people with them gave me a pat over the fence when I sniffed their front paws.

Mum had a special day while we were away and Granny got her a special present. It was all shiny and sparkly, but there was something even better inside it! She took the outside off and then there was a picture of me and Hare that someone had copied from the picture I sent you! It looked a bit different though - like it was soft and warm and a bit fuzzy - but it's really me and Hare. We like it very much.

I think I'm tired from all my travels so I'll stop now and tell you the rest later. I'm going to go to bed and dream about my holidays.

Goodnight Milo. Sleep well.

Your friend

Jackson

19th September 2021

Dear Milo

I hope you are well. I am very well although I think the dark is getting a bit longer. In the other place that usually meant that there was going to be less to eat but I hope that will be different here.

It has been quiet since my last letter, but I need to finish telling you about my holiday which seems like a long time ago now.

One day - the day before we came home - we went to a place that had the sea all around it. There was a big old house at one end and some little ones at the other. But there were lots and lots of people walking around and some of them had dogs but there were no other Pointers like me. There was a Labradoodle though, but he wasn't black like you. We went around the whole place and I was very good. There was lots of grass and amazing smells so I kept my nose down and my tail wagging the whole time. Every now and then other people would stop to talk to Mum and Dad even though they didn't know them, so I'd have to stop and come and sniff them to make sure everything was OK. I always got a cuddle when I did that so that was nice. I'm sending you a picture of me with the big old house. We didn't go in because dogs weren't allowed but I didn't mind.

After that we did something amazing - we had ice cream! Have you ever had ice cream, Milo? I never had it before so wasn't quite sure what to do at first but as soon as I gave it that first lick I couldn't get enough! It's cold and sweet and so, so yummy. Mum and Dad had ice creams too but theirs had a stick in it. Mine didn't. In the end Mum said I had had enough and I think she put the rest of my ice cream away for later although I haven't had it yet. I think ice cream is my favourite thing in the world now.

After that we went to the beach again, but this one was different. We had to walk an awfully long way to get there, and on the way we met some big cows and some little cows. I think Mum and Dad were a bit worried by the cows but I didn't pay any attention to them at all. I was more interested in trying to find where the bunnies were. I could smell them and could see the big holes they had dug and I think if I wasn't on my lead I could have caught one. But Dad held on tight and kept saying "With Me" so I wasn't allowed to go anywhere. Before we got to the beach there were lots of ups and downs made of sand and covered in long grass but I wasn't allowed on those either because there were birds sitting down. That was really hard and very unfair, I thought.

The beach was wonderful. It was so big I couldn't see the end and we were the only ones there so Dad and I went for a long run. Well, I went for a run anyway - mainly in big circles around Dad as he was holding the end of my long lead. I was very good again and nearly always went to him when he called me. In the end we went back to where Mum was sitting and after a rest (although I wasn't tired) we walked all the way back, through the place with the big and little cows, until we got to the car again where I got in and went straight to sleep.

Only one bad thing happened on my holiday and that was when we got back from the empty beach. While we went from the car to the house, I felt something little on my back and then it hurt! A lot! I yelped and tried to look but couldn't see what it was. Dad got very excited too and started waving his hand over me and then stamped his foot on something. Have you ever seen a wasp, Milo? They are small and stripey and angry and mean and will bite you even if you don't do anything to them. I don't like them at all. My back still hurt so Mum sat for ages with me in the grassy place and held something nice and cool against my back. I couldn't see what it was but it I think it might have been the rest of my ice cream which is sad. While we were there lots of people passed by and they all stopped to make sure I was OK. After a while it didn't hurt quite so much but I was feeling very sorry for myself so went to bed early.

The next morning we put everything back into the car again and drove for a long, long time. I went to sleep for a lot of it, apart from when we'd stop at big places with lots of cars and people where I'd go for a little walk and have a wee before getting back in again. I like the car, now that I'm with the people in the front. It's very comfy. In the end though, we stopped and I got out and realised we were home! I was very excited to be home and made sure I had a good sniff and a wee in all the important places.

When we went to see Uncle Reefing, he sniffed Dad from top to bottom to make sure he was OK and then turned his back! Apparently this is what he does when he's upset with Dad for going away without him. It didn't last long and he's fine again now.

My holidays were lovely and I had a wonderful time, but I am very happy to be home again. Different places and people and things are all good but I like being where I belong and where I fit, looking after my people and being part of my family.

It's funny though. Since getting home I think things are a little bit different and better. All the people I met were nice and kind so I am happier now when I meet strangers and don't worry as much. Today on my walk I met a new friend named Poppy. She's a spaniel and lives near me. Before my holiday I'd have been a bit scared of her but because I've met and played with so many dogs we started to play straight away and it was great!

Do you hear your people when they call you Milo? As you know, I don't always but I'm trying hard. Maybe if I was to visit you could show me what you do? I'd like very much if we could do that. It would be very exciting to meet you!

Until then, be a good boy and keep wagging!

Your friend

Jackson

27th September 2021

Dear Milo

Hello again!

It seems like an awfully long time since my holiday now, and the routine here at home has settled back to normal: stay in bed as long as I can and get up only when Dad makes me, have a walk, breakfast, back to bed, help Mum and Dad with their work, have another walk, lunchtime snooze, play Silly Boy outside, more work, late afternoon doze and then a big long walk before having dinner and going to bed. Things have been a bit strange here recently though. Some of the places in the house look a bit different – some of the lights are in different places and some of the wooden things have changed. I think I like my home exactly as it is and worry that if it changes too much it won't be my home anymore. I'm getting used to it now though and it's not too bad. At least my bed is in the right place and hasn't moved, although I have experimented a bit by bringing my blanket into the place where Mum works.

Something else strange happened the other day and I didn't like it at all. It was only for a little while but it made me quite unhappy. Mum and Dad went up the wooden hill, even though the sun was out, and when they came down again, they had different coats on.

Usually they look very light and bright and happy but this time they looked dark and sad and a bit scary. They reminded me of something that happened a long time ago in the other place and I got very frightened. I could hear their voices but I was too scared of what I was seeing so I ran away. When Mum came to find me she had changed and didn't look dark anymore so I gave a little wag although I was still worried and it took me a little while before I was ok. Mum and Dad went out then and neither of them were dark when they came home so I was very happy about that and gave them a great welcome.

I don't know why I'm scared of people who wear the dark. Sometimes you forget things until a little thing happens and then you remember how you feel but not why. I think Mum and Dad know now that I don't like it so they won't wear the dark anymore, and that's nice.

I've been working really hard on listening when we go outside now and am a Very Good Boy most of the time unless I forget. I still wear my long lead though, even though it would be so nice to be able to run without it. I kind of forgot for a little while after our holidays and Dad had to use the Boss Man voice a lot. I'm much better now though and keep trying my best.

When we go for our walks, I say hello to all the other dogs I meet when we are out and about. Most of them are very nice and polite - we have a little sniff and maybe a small bounce - but some don't seem to like me at all. These dogs are usually quite little, but very, very loud. Most of the time they are on a lead and very rude, pulling at their people and shouting at me. Rosie told me that it's not personal and that these little dogs don't like ANYONE and I shouldn't let it bother me so I usually ignore them and just carry on. There are some though that are never on a lead, no matter how often we meet them, and they always ignore their people when they call them. I don't like it at all, and I can see that Dad doesn't like it either, although he kind of smiles at the people and tries to be polite as he looks after me and pushes the little dogs away with his foot. I don't think they know any better, if I'm honest, so their people should really help them to learn to be polite and play nicely like everyone else. Until then I think they should stay on a lead so nobody gets upset.

I chased a bunny today! I didn't see him but I could smell that he had been in MY big grassy place behind the house, which was a bit of a cheek. I've been investigating the hedge very closely since then and I'm sure I'll catch him soon, just like I did with the mousey. I'll smell him, then I'll see him and then I'll point at him. I can't really remember what happens next but I'm sure something will come to me.

Poor Hare has had a terrible time and has lost her tail! I think Monkey took it and have been interrogating him very closely but he's not given anything up yet. I know it will turn up eventually and Mum will be able to do her magic and fix it. HedgePig has had some issues too. Apparently when we went on holiday he hid in a bag and didn't come out for ages. He's looking remarkably well rested though.

Uncle Reefing has now forgiven Dad for going away and they have been going for lots of runs together. He and Dad have been friends for a very long time and when they're out Dad tells him lots of stuff that I don't understand. Uncle Reefing says I have a very interesting time ahead of me and I have a lot of surprises coming my way. He looked happy when he said it though, so I'm sure they're going to be nice surprises. I'll tell you all about it when it happens.

Until then Milo, I'll say goodbye. Keep being a Good Boy and remember to be polite and friendly to all the other dogs you meet.

Your good friend

Jackson

*My therapist – A surprise visit – Going
backwards to go forwards – Expensive shoes*

Dear Milo

I hope you are well. It seems to be getting cold and wet again. Is this usual? I had to wear a coat yesterday as it was so wet. Hopefully it won't get any worse. I much prefer it when it's warm.

I've met a lot of new people and dogs since I last wrote. One day a lady came to our house. She was very nice and smelled of lots and lots and lots of different dogs. She had a magic bag like Mum and Dad's with yummy stuff in it. They sat talking for ages while I sniffed around, and kept looking at me and what I was doing. Then Dad picked up my lead so I got all excited as that means we're going for a walk.

Usually, when we go for a walk, I get to go first and tell Dad where to go. This time I wasn't allowed and had to stick by Dad even though he wasn't saying "With Me". Instead he said something like "eel" but I didn't see any. I got some yummy treats though so I was quite happy to walk beside him. When we got to the big grassy place and he put on my long lead things got even stranger. Usually I go to the very end and come back when the lead goes tight. This time though he didn't call to me until he was really close and I was told I was a Good Boy as soon as I turned my head when I heard my name. Then Dad started to run backwards which looked very funny so I ran after him, and got yummies when I caught him! It was a great game and we've played it a lot since then, although sometimes I get distracted by birds and don't always hear my name.

When we got home we played a new game called "On Your Bed". The rules seem to be that Mum says "On Your Bed" and I have to sit on my blanket and then I get something nice. Sometimes she says "Down" and moves the yummy thing until it's near the floor so I have to lie down to eat it. Then everyone says I'm a Good Boy and I get lots of cuddles. I like this game very much.

Afterwards, they all went and sat in the room I don't like which was really mean as they know I can't go in there. Usually they talk to me and tell me I'm a Good Boy when I won't go inside but this time nobody said anything! I walked back and forth outside and stopped to look in, but they completely ignored me and didn't look at me, even when I whined a bit and pulled my blanket out. Very strange.

Then everyone went back to the place where we eat and it was all cuddles and "On Your Bed" again until the nice lady left. I liked her very much and hope I'll see her again.

Uncle Reefing says this lady is my Therapist and will help me be a happier boy and make my new life even better. He says most of what she's doing is helping Mum and Dad to be better at looking after me. I think you should never be afraid to get help when you need it. It also seems to mean I get lots more yummy stuff so I'm very happy about that.

Today was very exciting as I met some more lovely people and lots of other Pointer boys and girls who also lived in the other place! We got in the car but instead of going to The Yard we went a little way further and as soon as I got out I saw the V.I.V who came to see me at my house and with her was a Pointer named Henri. He was nice but I think it will take a little while before we get to know each other properly so we both stayed on our short leads. Then we went through a gate into another grassy place and three other Pointers came out of a house to say hello! There was another boy and two girls. Sully is a liver girl and so is her daughter Tilly. Max is a brown flecked boy like me.

After we'd had a quick sniff we went for a walk with their Mum and Dad in a great big grassy place. Max and Sully and Tilly were running free but Henri stayed on his short lead and I was on my long lead. It was wonderful, although I think I spent too much time checking the hedges for birds and not enough time playing with the others. I hope they don't think I was rude.

After our walk we went and sat in the house which was lovely with a floor that was toasty warm on my tummy. I felt very happy there and sat by Mum while the people talked and talked and talked. I liked them all very much and hope that I see them all again very soon so we can play properly. Maybe they can come to my house so I can show them things like the tomato I'm pointing at in the picture I'm sending.

I really like going places now, so who knows where I'll go next!

Goodnight Milo. Be good and look after your house.

Your friend

Jackson

10th October 2021

Dear Milo

Well what a surprise that was! I had no idea when we got into the car this morning that we were going to visit you!

I'm sorry I was a little shy when we first met. Going new places and making new doggy friends is still sometimes a worry for me, and I really wanted you to like me so I was a bit nervous. It was really nice to play with you afterwards though, and thank you for being so generous with your toys. That game of chase was brilliant! It was great to be able to run around in your big grassy place and sniff stuff and see all the amazing things you have. Your Hare is very like mine, so I think they must be related. Hopefully your Monkey is better behaved than mine though, and I'm sure your new HedgePig will be very happy with you.

I really like your home. It's a long way away but it's very nice and happy. I particularly like the big bed on legs where the people sit. It was very comfy and I enjoyed my snooze, especially as I was able to rest my head on Dad. Did you see the way he gently tugs on my ears when my head is on his knee? I love that. Sadly we can't do it as much at home as our sitty down thing is in the place I don't like.

My people are still being a bit odd about that place at the moment. They insist on sitting in there, but no matter how much I walk up and down or peer in, they don't pay any attention to me - not even a look! I've even started pulling my blanket and my bed around the place just outside but they still don't react at all. I really don't know what to do next, but I it will have to be drastic, whatever it is.

I saw something on Dad's little people-box the other day that was very interesting. There was a little Pointer puppy sitting on some sand and the wind was blowing his ears up and down. Dad thought it was very funny but he wouldn't be laughing if he had proper ears like you and me. We both know how serious a problem Flappy Ear Flap can be.

Did you notice how good I am at listening? Whenever my name was called I went straight over and plopped my bottom on the ground. I was really trying to be on my best behaviour and make Mum and Dad proud of me. Did I do well? I think I did well. It's harder when we're out though, and especially now when there seems to be loads of birds around. I found a lovely pheasant the other day and made him fly ever so high. Dad was obviously very proud of me so I spent the rest of our walk looking for another one. He kept telling me how good I was. At least I think that's what he was saying. I wasn't really listening, to be honest, as I had more important things to do.

Thank you for being so nice to Mum and Dad. I didn't mind at all that they gave you cuddles and strokes and pulled your ears. I like your Mum and Dad very much too! They are very nice and I like especially that your Mum is little like mine. You are very lucky to have grown up with such wonderful people who love you so much. Take care of them, Milo. They are very very special.

Thank you again, Milo, for a lovely, lovely day. I'm so happy our people are friends and that we are too.

Goodnight, my friend.

Jackson

17th October 2021

Dear Milo

I hope you are well.

This will be just a short letter today as Dad is a bit poorly so Mum and I have to look after him. He's resting and taking medicine so he'll be all better soon.

I take medicine too. Mum gives me things that look like little pebbles wrapped up in cheese or some lovely nutty stuff that sticks to my teeth and lasts for ages because it takes so long to lick off. They're not really pebbles though. They're crunchy. Mum thinks I don't know what she's giving me, but I do. It's medicine to keep me well and happy. The medicine stops nasty bugs from living in my fur and in my tummy. We all need to take medicine sometimes. I think I told you the first time I took medicine for these bugs it actually made me very poorly, so the new medicine is better and I don't mind it at all. That happens sometimes. The medicine works but it can take a couple of tries to see what works best.

Sometimes the only thing that helps will make you feel bad for a little while, but you still have to take it. You should always take medicine when you can, because it helps you and everyone around you.

I didn't get any medicine at all when I lived in the other place. Maybe if I did, I wouldn't have some of my marks. Some of the other dogs I know over there were very poorly indeed, but nobody was there to help them and give them little pebbles wrapped in cheese. The Lovely Lady who helped me does, though. She helps lots and lots of dogs even though she doesn't have many pebbles. Uncle Reefing says I can help her get lots more, though. I don't understand how, but Uncle Reefing is very clever so if he says something it must be true.

Something wonderful arrived for me today! A very nice lady I know sent me a present. I didn't know what it was, as it was all wrapped up in exciting papery stuff but what was inside was even better - it was a tiny me! I knew it was me straight away because it has lots of the things that make me me - it has my face, and my paws and my spots and the big patch on my back and the blob on my bottom. Also, there was a teeny tiny Ducky and a little pile of the soft papery things that look like toys but aren't. I gave it all a good sniff and then let Mum put it somewhere safe where people can see it and say how handsome I am. I'm sending you a picture so you can see what it's like.

How are you getting on with your HedgePig? Mine got stuck under a wooden thing in the room where we eat, and I wasn't able to reach him with any of my paws so Mum had to help him out. I think Monkey must have dared him to go in there when I wasn't looking.

Uncle Reefing is very hairy now. He says it's because winter is coming. I think that's when it gets a bit colder and there's a bit less light. The nighttime is certainly longer now but I'm happy to sleep in my cosy bed. Apparently Uncle Reefing is due a haircut. I'm not sure what that is but it sounds very strange, so I'll tell you all about it when it happens.

Until then, Milo, keep taking care of your family and I will write again very soon.

Your good friend

Jackson

24th October 2021

Dear Milo

I hope you are well. I am very well thank you, although I think I ate something yesterday that disagreed with me as my tummy was a bit iffy today. I'm fine now though, and very much enjoyed my dinner tonight.

Mum and Dad are doing some odd things here at the moment. Mum took everything off the walls and moved all the stuff around in the place where they eat and piled it all in the middle. Then she and Dad opened this big can of stuff that smells really nasty and started putting it on the wall with some hairy things. I don't like that things are different so I stayed away and just looked in the door, but they were very busy. Mum seemed to stick to the bits that were low down because she's only little while Dad did the high bits. I came in to look once and wagged my tail but Dad shooed me out again and had to wipe my tail with a papery thing. They've stopped now and the place smells funny and I don't like that much, but it's very bright. They seem happy though, and that's the main thing.

I got stuck in a bush again the other day. As I was standing there waiting for Mum to come and get me out

I started to think: isn't it funny that sometimes in order to go forwards you have to go backwards first. To get out of this bush I had to reverse and wiggle my bottom quite a bit but then I was free and could go wherever I wanted. It's like that with a lot of things. If you want to learn something new then sometimes you have to forget something you already know and that's hard. In the other place, every time I went out I had to try to find birds. That's not my job now so I have to try to forget that and listen to Mum and Dad when they say my name. It's really hard and sometimes it makes me sad that I'm not very good at it, but Mum and Dad are there to help me. When I listen and look at them when they say "Jackson'" it makes them very happy and they give me a treat. I want to make them happy and I'm really trying, but it's awfully hard when there's so much to smell and see and search for. I'm going to keep doing my best and someday I'll make them really proud of me.

I did find a particularly nice ditch today mind. I'll show it to you when you come to visit. It has a lovely squelchy bottom. I'm sending you a picture so you can see a little bit of it.

There is a small shouty dog I often meet when we walk past her house. She makes an awful lot of noise when she sees us, running up and down behind her gate and pushing her nose under the fence as we pass. Well, the other day we met her and her Mum when we were both out for a walk and she was like a different dog! I mean, I still didn't go anywhere near her as she's still quite grumbly and little dogs scare me, but we had a perfectly civil conversation without any shouting at all. It would be lovely if we could all talk like this all the time without being scared of each other, because I think she's a little bit scared of me too.

I think I told you we have new neighbours? Well tonight one of the men came to our house and he brought me some presents! I was a bit woofy when he arrived, but I couldn't control my very waggy tail so I'm not sure he took me seriously, unfortunately. It seems he found a lovely water bowl that belonged to his dog Bijou and thought I might like it. Bijou had to go away a little while ago and I could tell he was sad thinking about her so I stopped woofing and went to him for some cuddles instead. That seemed to make him very happy. Then I tried to eat his shoe until Mum took it away, which was a shame as it tasted very expensive.

Uncle Reefing had the haircut he told me about and looks very smart, although he's a slightly different colour now. He and Dad can go for runs again without him getting too hot and that makes him very happy. He says I don't need a haircut though as I'll need all my fur to keep me warm during the cold that's coming.

Hare is very well, and she continues to be wonderful company. HedgePig on the other hand has had another slight accident but he has 3 other legs so I'm sure he'll be fine.

Say hello to your people for me, Milo. They are lovely and kind and you are lucky to have them.

Until next time

Your friend

Jackson

1st November 2021

Dear Milo

I'm so sorry I didn't write yesterday but Dad was late for absolutely everything yesterday and I got so confused I forgot what day it was! It was a very strange day anyway and we had some really odd visitors once it got dark. They were little people and they looked very strange and scary. Mum got excited when they made the bell ring and gave them stuff that smelled tasty but I wasn't allowed any. I had a bit of a woof at the first few but got bored after that so stopped and went to bed.

I was quite tired actually as we had a very busy day with lots of walks. It was very windy so even though Flappy Ear Flap was a problem, there were big piles of leaves to shove my nose into and there's always something interesting underneath. I got a little bit excited when we got to a puddle and went for a bit of a splashy

Do you remember Uncle Reefing had a haircut? The nice lady who looks after Uncle Reefing came to give Dad a haircut too. Dad sat down in the room where Mum makes food and the lady made these snippy noises around his head and his fur fell off! I thought this was really interesting and watched closely and even tried to taste the fur but Mum stopped me and took it away which was a bit mean. Dad looks very smart now though although his ears look a bit cold.

I went for a walk with Rosie the other day and that was lovely. I felt a bit sad though because I wasn't allowed to run around with her and had to stay on my lead. I'm getting much better at listening though. Most of the time now I look at Mum or Dad when they say my name, no matter where we are. It's still hard though, because there are more birds around now and they smell amazing, and today we met a great big deer! He jumped out of the hedge right in front of me and ran away really fast. I wanted to run too but Mum held tight to my long lead and made me stay. I kept looking for him afterwards but didn't see him again. I'll look again tomorrow in case he comes back.

There was a lot of noise tonight after it got dark. Lots of bangs way up in the sky. I didn't mind it as it reminded me a bit of what my old life was like in the other place when The Man pointed the big stick at the birds. I know that some dogs don't like it though, so hopefully it won't happen again.

I heard something sad today. There is an old lady pointer named Maddie who lives with another dog like me and the time came for her to go away. She was very lucky to have people who loved her very much and showed their love by helping her and staying with her until she was gone even though it made them very sad. That's what real love is. She taught my friend so much even though they didn't know each other for long, and she will always be remembered. She was a Very Good Dog.

One night lots of people came to our house. Luckily Mum had been very busy making noise and smells in the food place all day because they seemed very hungry and ate and ate until everything was gone. I was a bit unsure about having so many people there at first so stayed outside for a while until Mum brought me inside. I had a woof or two but soon saw that they were people I knew and it was all OK. I recognised the man from next door because of his tasty expensive shoes but Mum put them up high so I couldn't try them again. When Mum sat on the floor afterwards though I was able to come and sit with her and join in with everyone. They stayed for ages and I was very sleepy when they all went home.

I'm getting sleepy again now so I think I'll curl up I'm my bed. It's getting a bit cold at night now so I might even put on some pyjamas.

Goodnight Milo. Maybe you'll meet a deer in your dreams.

Your friend

Jackson

New friends in a new place – Cold and dark – A thorny problem

7th November 2021

Dear Milo

I hope you're well

I'm very well thank you, but my goodness so much has happened since I last wrote! I've made lots of new friends and met lots of new people and they have all been very nice.

One day Dad and I got in the car and went for a drive. It was just him and me and we went to meet a lady who lives in a big grassy place with a fence all around it. I liked her but when we got there I was more interested in sniffing around and seeing what I could find because Dad took my lead off! That's right - I was in this big place and I wasn't attached to anyone and could go anywhere I wanted. It was brilliant!

Then someone else arrived. I saw what looked like one of those big stripey cats jumping up and down behind a gate. But it wasn't a cat. It was a very bouncy stripey dog.

We had a sniff through the gate and then she came into the field and we met properly. Her name is Athena and she came from a hot place just like I did but she's been here longer than me.

Athena said that she and her Mum have lots of dogs come to visit them from time to time. Their Mums and Dads bring them and Athena's job is to look after them and play with them until their people come back again a little while later. That sounds like a great job! I really liked Athena and her Mum and would like to go back and see them again. I hope I do. Dad and Athena's Mum talked for an awfully long time, but I didn't mind because that meant that Athena and I could play for longer. In the end though, Dad called me and I went straight to him. This always seems to make him very happy. He put my lead on and we got into the car again.

We didn't go home though. Instead we drove for a little bit and got out in another place I didn't know. We went to an old house and a heard some woofing when we got to the gate. A man opened the door and a big black Labrador came out woofing. He looked at me, stopped woofing and went back inside. Then he came back out again carrying a toy! His name is Scooby and now he's my friend. He's very old but he likes to play. I was a little bit shy to start with but was soon happy to talk to him. He's taught me how to woof AND carry a toy at the same time.

Then we went to his grassy place with big walls while Dad and the man sat down talking and drinking stuff. I met another dog here. Her name is Meera and she's a Husky. I've never met a Husky before. They're very fluffy. Dad and his friend let us take our time and get to know each other which was nice. She was quite friendly but not like Scooby who was very happy to meet me. I had a lovely time sniffing around their grassy place and playing with my new friends until Dad said it was time to go home.

That was a lovely day and I think Dad was proud of me because I was very brave and went to all these new places and met all these new friends and I wasn't scared. I hope I'll meet all of them again very soon.

Another day, Rosie came to my door just after we had breakfast. She had her Dad with her and he was carrying bowls and a lead and smelly food and lots of stuff. He said something to Mum and then he left. Rosie was as surprised as me, I think, as she stayed at the door for a little while before coming to talk to me. Then she stayed for ages and ages and it was brilliant! We played for most of the day except for when we had a snooze or when we went for a walk. Rosie got a bit bored on our walk, I think. She doesn't like birds or sniff about as much as I do.

Rosie did an amazing thing though. She went straight into the scary place and climbed up on the big bed on legs that Dad was sitting on! I was still too scared and although I looked in at them I wasn't able to go in. Rosie doesn't understand why I'm scared and I don't think I really do either. I don't know if I'll ever go in there.

In the end, when it was very late and time for bed, Rosie wanted to go home. She was missing her Mum and Dad and wanted to be in her own house, so she was happy when there was a noise at the door and they came to get her. I was sad to see her go but it was nice not to have to share Mum and Dad any more.

I think I'm much happier meeting other dogs again now. I've been a bit nervous since the unpleasantness with Bertie but although I still like to take a little time, we start to play much more quickly now. I get very excited when we meet other dogs on our walks and jump around a lot. Don't tell anyone, but today I jumped around so much I actually fell over! I was very embarrassed but I don't think anyone saw.

It's been such a busy time I almost didn't notice the big bangs in the sky tonight. I had a good old bark at them, but wasn't scared at all and wagged my tail the whole time. They were very loud but I kept our house safe from them and looked after Mum and Dad the whole time.

It's tiring though, so I'm off to my bed now for a good sleep. I hope you sleep well too.

Your good friend

Jackson

14th November 2021

Dear Milo

I hope you are well.

Is it getting colder and darker where you are? It is here. A while ago we used to go for a long walk at the end of the day but now it happens in the middle or sometimes even at the start. Sometimes now it's actually dark when we go out. We don't go on the grassy bit when it's dark. Instead we use the hard bit where the cars go, although we don't see very many of those. Everyone can see me though! Dad put a very bright light on my clippy strappy thing and when it's dark you can see it from a really long way away. He wears a bright coat and carries something that makes another big light and helps us see where we're going. I like going out because my nose helps me know where I am all the time. I think Dad struggles a bit though, as his nose is a bit...well, it's a people nose - you know what I mean.

We do have a game I love though. You know the way our people pick up poo? When we go out in the dark I try to make sure I poo in the most difficult, darkest place possible so they have to scrabble around to find it! It's great fun. Recently I've taken to doing it outside the big house where Welly lives because that's really awkward.

Do you think people know how important our noses are? They seem to rely very much on what they see but you and I know how much they're missing. The other day Dad came downstairs really early and I was asleep and didn't hear him. I smelled him though. But he didn't smell like himself. He smelled of something that reminded me of the other place when The Man would put me in the car with the other dogs and go looking for birds. I was scared and worried so I growled and barked until I came out of my bed and saw it was Dad. I still didn't like it mind, and wasn't sure what was happening so it took a while before I wagged my tail again. He smelled amazing when he came home again though! Of birds and dogs and trees and dirt and all kinds of good things.

I have decided I don't like the wet. It's strange - in the other place, whenever it rained, I got wet. Whenever it was cold, I got cold. Now, I think Mum and Dad would do absolutely anything to keep me dry and warm. And happy. I think they want me to be happy so I'm trying to make them happy too. I still have days when I'm scared or when I worry a little bit about new things or something reminds me of the other place, but I think I'm happy now.

Do you like your food Milo? I ask because of something that happened when Rosie was here. She had her dinner of smelly chicken, and then when Mum wasn't looking she stood on her back legs and shoved her nose straight into my dinner! I hadn't had it yet so it was sitting up high. She really loves her food and will try to eat anything she can reach, even if it's people food. Food isn't really that important to me, to be honest. I mean, I like treats (who doesn't?) but I'm not one of those dogs that will do anything for a biscuit. Sometimes I wonder if it might be easier if I did but then I wouldn't be me.

I've learned some new things since last time. My new favourite is "Down". Mum says "on your bed" so I go into my bed or onto a blanket. Then she says "sit" but most of the time I've already done that. Then she says "Down" so I move my front legs forward until I'm flat on the ground and then I get told I'm a Very Good Boy and get a lovely treat and lots of cuddles. I'm really good at Down.

I can see Mum is putting stuff into a bag and I think I should help, so I'm going to finish now.

Goodnight Milo. Stay warm and dry.

Your friend

Jackson

p.s. Apparently HedgePig is going to do something called "retire" as he's afraid he'll lose more bits...

22nd November 2021

Dear Milo

I hope you are well and staying warm. For my morning walk today the grass was crunchy and really cold under my paws! Is it like that where you are? I'm sending you a picture of me with some crunchy leaves.

Since I last wrote I've been very happy and very sad and everything in between. It's been quite strange.

After my last letter, Mum got up in the middle of the night and carried some bags outside. Then she came back, gave me a cuddle (I was very sleepy) and went back out again. I went back to sleep but she hadn't come back when the light came and I woke up. I looked for her for a bit, but Dad took care of me and made me feel better. Then later, I saw where she had gone - she was in Dad's people box! It sounded like her and looked like her but she was very very small. It was all very confusing.

Then one day Dad got me up very early and instead of going for our walk, we got in the car. We drove for a while and when we stopped we were at the place where I met Athena (the tiger dog who came from a hot place like me) and her nice lady. Athena wasn't there but Dad gave my coat and bag of yummies to the lady and then gave her my lead. I wasn't sure what was happening but went with her and had a sniff. Dad was still there watching so I sniffed a little more and walked a little further. And then, when I looked around, I couldn't see Dad. He was gone!!

I was very sad and scared and got very upset. I thought Dad wasn't going to come back. I thought I didn't have my home anymore and that I had nobody to love me. I thought I was going to go back to the other place. So do you know what I did, Milo? I went to the big door where I last saw Dad and I sat and cried. I cried and cried. The nice lady gave me cuddles but that wasn't what I wanted. I wanted my Dad.

The lady kept cuddling me but started saying something to the little box that people carry. So we sat there - me crying and the lady talking. We sat there for what seemed like ages and ages and ages and then a wonderful thing happened. I saw a car and then Dad got out! I was so very happy to see him. I jumped and bounced and wagged my tail so very hard.

Dad gave me big cuddles while he talked to the lady and then we went and got in the car again but we didn't go straight home. On the way we stopped at a huge big shiny house where Dad went in and then came out carrying some of the papery things he looks at when he's talking on the people box during the day. I met loads of people while we were there. Nice men and ladies who came out to the car where I was waiting and gave me cuddles and talked to Dad. I knew some of them because I saw them before on the people box. One of them was Jack's mum so now I know what he smells like! Then Dad got into the car again and we went straight home.

I don't think I've ever been so sad as I was when I thought I was alone again. But he came back. My Dad came back for me. I think he will always come back for me. And I will always wait for him.

I met the other nice lady - my therapist - again too. She came early one morning and we had a lovely time. We went for a walk and I showed her all the things I've learned - how not to pull on my lead, how I can go on my bed and lie down and how much better I am at listening to Mum and Dad when we're out. We played a great game with Monkey too. She held him up and squeaked him and threw him so I could chase after and pick him up. It was SO exciting! Then when I brought him back, she said "Off" and when I put him on the floor I got a yummy. Then Dad did the same and I got really good at it. Sometimes Monkey landed near the room I don't like so I'd have to sneak my head in to pick him up. I was very brave.

I would have liked to play that game with HedgePig but I can't find him. I've looked everywhere but I don't know where he could be. I'm very worried and hope he's ok.

But later something else wonderful happened. After two sleeps, Mum came home again! It was late and dark and I was asleep when she came but she came home too. She smelled a bit funny - kind of like when I had to go up in the air to come here - so I was unsure at first. Then after a little while she came back and she was damp but she smelled like Mum again and I was so happy I couldn't help but bounce around and play Silly Boy even though it was after bedtime.

So that's it, Milo. It has been a very eventful time for me. We're all here together again and I know now that Mum and Dad will always come back and I will always be waiting for them, wherever we are. All I need now is to find HedgePig and everything will be perfect.

Goodnight Milo. I hope you find some lovely interesting things to sniff.

Your friend

Jackson

29th November 2021

Dear Milo

Well, it's been another exciting time since I last wrote!

Rosie came to stay again for a whole day which was lovely. We got to run and play together for ages. We even got to play Tug with my rope, which was great because I love that game but Mum and Dad don't play it with me. It was odd again around food time though - Rosie really loves her food. She pushed past Mum to get into the place where my food lives and then she tried to get up to the high place where the people food is! She even took my chewy stick when she had finished her own one. I didn't mind though because I'm not that fussed about them. I DID get upset when she took t'Donkeh though, and wouldn't give him back. I whined until Mum got him back for me and gave Rosie one of her own toys.

She told me my eye looked a bit funny, and it actually did feel a bit wet and itchy. Ella told me the same when I met her and so did Lola. I suppose I shouldn't have been surprised then when we got in the car yesterday that we didn't go to our usual place but instead when we stopped I saw we were at the V.E.T. A very nice lady who sounded a lot like Dad came to the car, said I was a great lad and looked at my eye. Then she took me into the house where she lives and I was very brave and went with her even though Dad stayed outside. Another lady came to help then, and I got up on a high place and they poked around my eye A LOT! They put coloury stuff in that came down my nose and made me sneeze and then then shined a bright light in my face. I didn't like it.

The nice lady looked worried then and she brought me back outside where Mum and Dad were waiting for me. I was glad as I wanted to go home. Mum and Dad looked worried now, but we got back in the car anyway and drove for ages and ages but when we stopped we still weren't home. Instead we were actually at another V.E.T. house! You know how they smell of dogs and cats and wee and other smelly things? That's how I knew where we were even though I'd never been there before. A nice man came out to see me and told me I was a lovely boy. Then (I was very brave again) he brought me into his house where I stood in another high place and had more coloury stuff down my nose and more light in my face. The lady who was helping gave me lots of cuddles and played with me, and before I knew it the man had scrunched up his face and shoved something in my eye.

Then he took it out again very slowly and attached to the end of it was a great big stick! At least it felt like a great big stick, but it only looked like a little speck when he

171

got it out. My eye was a bit stingy but started to feel much better and not so itchy. I got lots of cuddles then and felt very brave and good. I kept thinking about how brave Apollo was when his eyes were sore and that helped me a lot. I'm sending you a picture of the stick.

I was very waggy to see Mum and Dad afterwards when we went back out into the cold. It was dark then and they were wearing coats and you could see their breath in the air. I got loads more cuddles and hugs and when Mum and Dad finished talking to the nice man we got back in the car and went on the long drive home.

On the way, we stopped at The Yard to see Uncle Reefing and make sure he was warm and had enough dry grass to eat. He thinks I probably got a thorn in my eye when I was looking for birds in the bushes and I need to be more careful. He said I should wear doggles on my face which he seemed to think was hilarious. I could still hear him saying "doggles" to himself and laughing when we were leaving.

I was very glad to get home and see my bed that night, although Mum has twice since poked her finger in my eye with some smelly stuff on it. Doesn't she know I've been poorly?!?

When Rosie was here the man who comes to the door most days to give me biscuits and give papery things to Mum and Dad brought a box for me. It was very exciting! Apparently it's from Apollo's Mum and has wonderful things inside it but I'm not allowed to see them yet. Rosie says it's for Kiss-Miss. I don't know what that is and Rosie won't tell me. She says I'll have to wait and see. If I know Rosie it probably has something to do with food.

I'm very worried about HedgePig. I haven't seen him for ages and he wasn't very well then, either. His nose had fallen off again and some stuff was coming out. I hope he's OK.

Milo, please tell me that it doesn't get any colder over here. I'm freezing! If I have to go outside I wear my big coat and come back inside as soon as I can. When I'm in bed I wear my pyjamas and snuggle under blankie until the light comes. I love my bed.

Mum and Dad haven't gone anywhere since the last time which is nice. Do your people go out without you, Milo? They always come back, don't they. I like that they always come back to us.

Anyway, enjoy your lovely home Milo. Take care of your lovely people, stay warm and keep your eyes out of the bushes.

Your good friend

Jackson

Stars on houses – What is Kiss-Miss? – A wonderful return

5th December 2021

Dear Milo

I hope you are well.

My eye is much better now, thank you very much. Mum wouldn't leave it alone and kept fiddling and poking at it and putting stuff in it so I'm surprised it got better at all. Anyway, we went back to the V.E.T. the other night and after putting more coloury stuff down my nose and shining the bright light in my face again, I was all fixed! I'm very lucky that Mum and Dad have such clever friends that were able to help me. To say thank you, Mum gave them a small flat plasticky thing from her pocket that made a little box go beep, and that was that.

When I lived in the hot place, I didn't have anybody to help me, so if I felt poorly I tried to be brave and hoped that things got better on their own because if I made a fuss then The Man got angry. When my eye started to hurt, I thought it was the same here so I stayed quiet.

Uncle Reefing says I shouldn't do that anymore. He says that if you're poorly or something hurts or if you just feel bad you should always tell someone. Because I have a family now, there is always someone who will help me feel better. And because Mum and Dad and Uncle Reefing are my family, I'll help them if they need it too. That's what you do for the ones you love. You help each other.

The grass has been very crunchy again, even though the sun has been nice and bright. I think I like going for walks when it's like that. Everything is very sharp and clean and when things get a little warmer you can smell where the birds and the mousies have been and their scent hangs just above the ground like a little puddle of lovely things and you just lose yourself in it. In the other place, when the nights got very long like they are now, it got cold too, but not as cold as here. I'm very glad to have a nice warm bed in my lovely home and think I'm very lucky.

I'm still learning lots of things. Dad and I practice "Wait" when we're out. I sit down and then he holds out his front paw and says the word, and then he steps back from me. I have to stay where I am then, and not move until he comes back to me and gives me something yummy and makes a big fuss and tells me I'm a Good Boy. I got distracted the other day though, by a big car in the sky that was very low and looked like a huge fly and made a lot of noise. I stayed where I was but forgot to look at Dad but he still said I was a Good Boy anyway.

There is something strange going on around here and I'm not quite sure what it is. When we go for our walk in the dark some of the houses have bright stars all over them that flash and sparkle, and there's more of them every time. Is that happening near you too? Mum and Dad have put two big trees in a bucket of water outside our house. The trees look like they're all wrapped up in a cobweb but it's not a cobweb and it smells funny. Uncle Reefing says we have to get presents for Mum and Dad for some reason and I have no idea how to do that. He says it's for Kiss-Miss, like Rosie said, but he won't tell me what it is either. He says I'm going to like it though.

The nice man who comes to the door every day with biscuits for me and papery things for the people brought something interesting too! It's called a Call-ender and it goes on the wall and tells you when to do things like take your medicine or go on holidays or buy cheese. It has a story that I told in it and lots of numbers and lots and lots of pictures of dogs like me. It's lovely and if people get them then more dogs will be able to find wonderful new homes like mine and not be sad anymore.

HedgePig still hasn't come home so I'm going to have one last look in the garden before I go to bed. Maybe he'll be home tomorrow. I hope so.

Goodnight Milo. Wish me luck.

Your friend

Jackson

12th December 2021

Dear Milo

I hope you are well. Dad showed me a picture of you on his people-box and your new haircut looks very smart indeed! I especially like the stylish coloury cloth around your neck. I've never had a haircut and I don't know if I'd like it. I have mixed feelings about even being brushed, to be honest. Dad makes it a game where I lie on my bed and wriggle while he tries to brush my back and then I try to get the brush and then he moves it to my side or my bum or my tummy and then I try to get it there. Sometimes I get his paw instead of the brush but I'm only playing so I don't bite or hurt him.

Life has been good here. Mum packed her box on wheels and went in the car in the middle of the night again. I think she goes to see the people in her people-box who live a long way away. She didn't come back for two sleeps and I was very happy to see her when she got home, even though she smelled funny. Dad and I missed her very much, and Dad rushed around washing things and putting them away before she came home.

I hope you're still enjoying your walks, Milo. We have our long walk in the middle of the day now, because of the dark. It's not as nice as having it early or just before the sun goes, but the lovely scent is still there and I still get the chance to look for birds. I found a very nice one today but had to Leave It and Come Out sadly. I think Dad is worried I'll hurt my eye again if I go into the bushes but I'm sure it will be fine.

I'm getting really good at Heel now, even when I don't get a treat. When they say it I walk very politely beside my person and hardly pull on the lead at all until they say Off You Go and then I can go for a run. I still have to wear the long lead though, just to keep me safe. I don't mind it too much, but it would be lovely to be able to run without it, even just for a little bit.

I have some new friends! Pepper and Copper are two other Pointers like me who heard I was worried about HedgePig so they sent me a box to help me feel better. It was a lovely box but what was inside was even better! Inside was a new ball, a little dog named Husky and a great big relative of HedgePig who smells like flowers. I've named him BigPig and love him and Husky very much. They are wonderful company, but Monkey is sulking and won't come down from the hot white wall. I still haven't heard from HedgePig which makes me very sad. I hope he's OK.

Do you remember I told you about how twinkly stars have appeared on houses around here? Well now it's happened to ours too! We went for a walk today and it was dark when we got back and there were stars all over the front and a bit of a bush on the door. It was very pretty but a little bit scary at first. It's fine now though. It's home and that's what's important.

I'm getting a bit concerned about this Kiss-Miss thing. Apparently, according to Uncle Reefing, I have to get a present for Mum and for Dad. What's that all about? The only things I know how to get are birds and the last time I gave one to Mum she didn't seem to like it very much. Uncle Reefing says not to worry as it kind of just happens but it's all very confusing. Everyone seems to be looking forward to it very much though...

Give your Mum and Dad a cuddle and take care of them, Milo. Be good.

Your friend

Jackson

19th December 2021

Dear Milo

I hope you are well, and I'm very happy you like your Call-ender. You need to put it somewhere lots of people can see it so it helps all those other dogs like me who are looking for happy homes. If you really like it, you can get another one from the lovely Apollo's Angels who rescued me.

It was very nice to see you and your Mum and Dad on the people box the other day. Did you see the other dogs with their people too? I think they all live with people your Mum and my Dad know from a long time ago. I'd like to go and visit them but I think we'd have to go up in the air to get to them and I wouldn't like that.

Milo, there is a huge big tree in our house! An actual real tree! It was sitting outside in a bucket for a little while but today Dad brought it inside, planted it in a little pot, and took the stuff-like-spiderweb off it. Then all the branches popped out and a load of stuff fell onto the floor. I tried to help but instead Mum asked me to go outside and when I came back the tree was covered in twinkly stars and glittery balls and toys. They look a bit like toys, anyway, but it's been made very clear to me that I'm not allowed to play with them yet. And under the tree is a box that I've seen before. It's the box that Apollo's mum sent to me a little while ago. I've only been allowed to take out one thing - a little version of me to hang in my tree - but the rest of it smells amazing!

Dad and Monkey and I went for another drive the other day and ended up at Athena's house again. If you remember, the last time I was there Dad drove away without me and I got very upset until he came back. I was a bit worried at first this time too, but Dad stayed nearby the whole time. Athena's Mum is very nice and took me for a little walk in her big field but I spent all my time looking for mousies and checking where Dad was. In the end a little white dog named Scotty came outside and Athena's Mum took my lead off so I could run around with her. I'm afraid I was a little bit rude, Milo. I ignored the little dog and kept looking for mousies and birds (although I didn't find any). It got very exciting when the lady started squeaking Monkey's nose, though. She threw Monkey in the air and then I'd run and get him and bring him back. And then she threw my rope and when I brought it back she played tug with me! I loved it because people don't usually play tug with me so she must be very special. After a bit, when I'd had a good run around and had a little bit of sausage, Dad and Monkey and I got back in the car and went home. I had a lot of fun and think maybe that place isn't so bad after all. When we got home I discovered that BigPig's nose fell off while I was away, sadly. I think it's a family thing, but Mum is helping him.

The grass was crunchy again today which reminded me of something. In the other place, at this time when the nights are really long and dark and the ground is really cold, something used to happen at The Man's house. Even though it was cold and dark outside in my little house, for one day The Man's house would be bright and warm and lots of other people would come. Some of them would carry boxes inside, and I could hear them singing and laughing and could smell wonderful things on the air. I never got to see what it was like of course, because I would never dare go into The Man's house - that would be far too scary. In any case, the day was always the same for me whatever happened - I lay on the ground in my cold tin house, with the heavy chain around my neck. I remember one time though when The Man threw some crunchy bones to me. They tasted wonderful and I had a full tummy and was happy for a little while. Then we went looking for birds and I must have done something wrong again because he got very angry with me.

It feels a little bit like that time again now, but I'm not scared or hungry anymore. I really like my tree - it's beautiful and exciting. I only wish HedgePig was here to see it. Uncle Reefing says this is a time for wishes, so that was going to be mine at first. When I thought about it though, it seemed selfish to use my wish just for me, so instead I wish that all the other dogs like me can find homes like mine and be happy and have their own people to look after and to love.

Goodnight Milo. Be happy and use your wish well.

Your good friend

Jackson

26th December 2021

Dear Milo

Merry Kiss-Miss!

I know what it is now! It's been such an exciting time since I last wrote.

You know that sparkly tree that I was telling you about? Well, lots of coloury boxes kept appearing under it until there were lots and lots of them, big ones and little ones and some that smelled really really good.

One day Mum put some of them into a big bag and we all got in the car and went to a new place where some people that Mum has known for a long time live. The coloury boxes are called Kiss-Miss presents and have wonderful things in them and you give them to the ones you love. I was wearing a new Kiss-Miss jumper for our visit, and everyone said I looked very smart and was a Very Good Boy. While we were there I made a new friend on the people-box! Her name is Clic and she is a very elegant lady who lives in a hot dry place with Mum's friend. The place is called Do-Buy and is even hotter and drier than the place I came from. Like me, she didn't have a real home until some lovely people helped

186

her and now she lives with her Mum and looks after her. She's very clever and says we've both won the lottery but I don't know what that means.

In the end, Mum gave her coloury boxes to her friends and they gave us some different ones instead to bring home and put back under our tree.

I was very tired that night and went straight to bed, although Mum and Dad stayed up for ages putting stuff on the table and mixing things in the food room and putting even more presents under the tree and drinking fizzy water. Then they put a glass of something and a little cake next to the burny thing, gave me a cuddle and a kiss, and went up to where they sleep. I slept very well and didn't move until Dad stroked my head the next morning.

My goodness Milo, but what a morning that was! I don't know how it happened but the glass and the little cake were gone, and a lovely soft sock had somehow appeared over my bed with presents in it. Dad took one out and I snuffled at it and licked it and touched it with my paw and a bit of the paper came off and then another bit and then picked it up in my mouth and lots of paper came off and then I was holding a beautiful new collar! It was a present from Uncle Reefing so we put it on and put on my jumper and then went to The Yard to wish him a Merry Kiss-Miss.

We met everyone there. Lola had a new jumper too but said she didn't like it and refused to put it on. She can be extremely wriggly when she wants. Then I had a great bounce around Uncle Reefing's field with Mum while Dad cleaned his house and then we went home again. Before we left I thanked him for my new collar and he thanked me for the big bag of treats I got him, which was a bit of a surprise to me if I'm honest.

When we got home, Mum and Dad poured out more fizzy water and we all sat next to the big tree and started opening presents. I think I got more than anyone! I got another new jumper and a new coat and yummy things and so many TOYS! My cousin Mario who lives in the place Dad came from sent me Raccoon who has a wonderful squeak and the nice lady who lives near here with the big tall man gave me Swan and Duckella and Fezzietoo and DifferentDuck and they are all wonderful. Clic sent me a squeaky thing called a cracker and there was a big sausage on a rope and lots of things.

But the most wonderful thing of all was sitting right in the tree. I heard that familiar squeak and looked up and there he was. It was HedgePig with a ribbon around his...well, his tummy, I suppose as he doesn't really have a neck. But it was him and I was very happy and excited to see him. He looks a bit different after his holiday and I have to be very careful with him now but my friend is back and that makes me very happy.

Later on some more people I know came to our house and Mum brought out the biggest chicken I have ever seen and it smelled amazing. The people sat for ages drinking even more fizzy water and ate lots and lots of the chicken and other food. I tried a little piece of it too and it was very nice.

Later on Rosie came to say hello and we had a lovely play together. She says the big bed on legs is called a "sofa" and she came and sat on it with Dad and me. I was Very Good and sat quietly but she got very excited and jumped on Dad giving him licks and kisses until she got told off. Again. Dad didn't mind though and laughed a lot.

We all slept a lot today, although Uncle Reefing actually came to our house to say hello. Dad was sitting on his back and they made an awful lot of noise as they trotted down the road. Sometimes I forget that Uncle Reefing is very big and he can be a bit scary. Kind of like Kiss-Miss. There were some lovely bits and it was all very exciting but I got a little scared sometimes when there was a lot of noise or new people or things looked different. Mum and Dad looked after me though. I think they know that it takes time for dogs like me to get used to things and they help me stay happy.

The presents and yummy food and everything were great, but the thing that made me happiest was having HedgePig home. I think that's what Kiss-Miss is for. To be with the ones you love, wherever they are. Even if HedgePig wasn't home I'd still love him and he'd still know that I loved him, wherever he was. Sometimes even if we can't be together in the same place, we can be together in our hearts. We can always be together in our hearts.

Goodnight Milo. Merry Kiss-Miss.

Your good friend

Jackson

A big new step – Time with Dad – The idea of a dog

January 2nd 2022

Dear Milo

I have huge news!

The other day, when Dad and I went on our long walk, I didn't have a lead or long rope or anything on at all! It was amazing. I was completely loose and free to go wherever I wanted without being attached to Dad or getting the rope tangled around me or anything. I was Very Good though, and stayed nearby and kept listening and went back to him whenever he called me. You would not believe the cuddles and treats I got.

We had been walking for quite a while before this happened mind you, and were headed for home the way we usually go. I had had a really good run around on the long rope and looked for birds for a bit. I found two pheasants and two hares so that was a lot of fun too. When we were around halfway home, as I was wandering along beside Dad, he stopped and asked me to sit down. I was paying a lot of attention to him so I plopped my bum on the ground straight away. Normally when we do this it's to swap over from the short lead to the long one or the other way round, but this time he just took the line off my clippy strappy thing, told me to wait, and stepped back. Then he said "Off you go". Normally when he says this I run off, but he looked a bit worried so I went over to check on him instead. He patted my head and smiled and told me I was a Good Dog so I knew then everything was ok.

We walked on for a bit and I had a little run around and a sniff, but Dad kept talking to me and every now and again he'd call me over and give me something yummy and then let me run off again. Eventually he called me back and asked me to sit down again and clipped my lead back onto my collar. I didn't mind because I could see he was very happy and very proud of me. I was proud of me too, because I listened and paid attention and didn't get distracted. I was a Very Very Good Boy.

I've lived in my home for a long time now - since the grass started to grow - and this is the first time I've been allowed to run around outside without being attached to Mum or Dad. Uncle Reefing says that's because dogs like me can get lost very easily if we're not sure where our home is or we don't know yet who our new Mum or Dad is. Sometimes it's because we get distracted and keep looking for birds and sometimes it's because bad people take us away. That can happen especially if you're very handsome like me.

When I think about it, Dad had worked it out very carefully when he decided to let me go without a lead. We had already had a long walk and I was a bit tired. We were close to home and I knew where we were going. There were no big roads nearby and I had the little box that goes "beep" on my collar. I always have that on whenever we go outside. I think he knew I might get distracted and not hear him, but he knew he'd be able to find me if we got separated. He still looked very relieved at the end though, and I'm glad I made him happy.

Did you get new ears yesterday? Everybody was saying it so I was wondering if I've missed out. I still have my old ears and thought maybe new ears would make me better able to hear Mum and Dad when we're out and about. Oh well, happy new ears to whoever got them anyway.

We had Gracie's Mum and Dad come and sit in the food place with my Mum and Dad and they stayed up really late which was a bit annoying as I wanted to go to bed. I don't remember anyone staying so long in our house before because when I woke up when the light came they were still there! They are nice and I like them so it's ok, although I still miss Gracie.

I went to visit Rosie in her house again today. I was a bit shy and didn't want to play at first. My tummy was a bit iffy (and whiffy!) but everyone thought it was Dad so I think I got away with it. Rosie and I had a lovely play then and we had great fun wrestling and playing bitey-face.

Now that the longest darkest night has been, things are going to get much nicer, I think. The sun will soon come back and things will start to grow again. There is always hope, Milo. Even when things are darkest we must always hope because tomorrow is another chance for things to be better.

Sleep well Milo. Have a good long run in your dreams.

Your friend

Jackson

p.s. HedgePig's nose fell off again so now he lives on a shelf above my bed where I can see him but have to ask before I can play with him. It's probably for the best.

January 9th 2022

Dear Milo

It's all change here again!

I was just getting used to having sparkly trees and ribbons and presents in the house and stars all over the front, and now they have all disappeared again. Mum and Dad spent ages taking everything down and carefully putting them into boxes. The boxes are still here, mind you. One in particular looks very suspicious so I had a good bark at it until I was told to get On My Bed. Which I did, of course, because I'm a Good Boy. I'm sure the boxes will disappear eventually too. Uncle Reefing says they will come back when the nights get really long and dark again, but for now we can look forward to the sun coming back again and everything being bright and warm.

That reminds me a bit of me, really. In the other place, I was cold and hungry and scared, but I was lucky and got a chance to start again and to change things and now I'm warm and my tummy is full and I'm not scared anymore.

I think the sun coming back reminds people that things can get better and then they work harder to change. You don't need the sun for that though. You can change and be better anytime you want, and there will always be friends to help you do it.

I do hope the warm comes back though as it's been really cold in the meantime. We've had a few more mornings with crunchy grass and I've had to wear my pyjamas AND have blankie at bedtime. Mum puts it on me when she goes to bed and it stays there until Dad gets me up to go for a walk the next morning. I like blankie and have only chewed it a little bit. Speaking of chewing, do you find that your toys' noses are the best part? Both HedgePig and BigPig have lost theirs, and now Raccoon's is quite soggy. Mum is very good at sorting them out though, so that's nice.

Mum and I saw something sad and scary yesterday. We were out walking really early and we saw a big car far away with men in it driving across the field. And there were dogs! Dogs running next to and in front of the car. Dogs kind of like my greyhound friends Izzy and Rosy. And I could tell they were looking for hares. It made me sad because even in the other place, when the stick went bang and the birds fell down, they were turned into food, but here I could see the men only wanted to see the hares being hurt.

I don't think I have ever seen Mum so angry, Milo. We didn't go near the men, but she started talking to the little box that she carries. Very soon afterwards the man that takes care of the land came to talk to us, and then a big car with flashy lights arrived. I didn't like that much but the people in it talked to Mum and very quickly went away in the same direction as the men and the dogs. I hope the dogs are ok, because I've met men like that before. They are not good men and I think the people Mum was talking to try to stop them from hurting animals and hurting other people. Rosie told me later that she saw a picture of some dogs in the back of the car with flashy lights, so I hope they get a chance to start again like I did and get a nice home with a soft bed where they will have a full tummy and be loved like I am.

I have been walking without a lead again since I last wrote, although I got a bit carried away one day and didn't hear Dad calling until he grabbed my collar and I had to wriggle backwards out of the prickly bush while he said his special words. Uncle Reefing says I have to make up for it as I've Blotted My Copybook. I have no idea what he's talking about, but I'm back on the long line again sadly.

Do you dance, Milo? I do. My dancing makes Mum laugh and I love that. I'll have to show you next time I see you.

In the meantime, be good and take care of your people. They don't need to get any better, but help them anyway if they think they do.

Your good friend,

Jackson

January 16th 2022

Dear Milo

I hope you are well and have had a nice day.

I had a lovely day today. Mum has gone oop north to help Granny so Dad and I have to look after each other for a little bit. We went for a long walk today and I was even off the lead for a while. I was very good and stayed close to Dad and listened to him. He doesn't do very well when Mum's not here so I'm taking good care of him until she comes home.

For a little while it felt like the growing time was starting. You know what I mean - now is the cold and dark time, so soon it will be the growing time and then the hot time and then time to rest before it gets cold and dark again. The last time it was like this - between the dark and the growing - was when I first met the Lovely Lady who rescued me. My life in the other place seems like a very long time ago and sometimes I even forget what it was like, but I will never forget the day I met my Apollo's Angel.

It started like all other days. I hadn't been given any food so I was hungry and cold in my tin shed. It had been raining so the ground was a little bit wet and I could see The Man talking loudly with another man and they were pointing at me. The Man was unhappy and that usually meant bad things for me so I was scared. I had often heard The Man shouting before but had never before seen the lady who was walking towards me. She was gentle and her voice was kind as she knelt down beside me. She stroked my head and called me a Poor Boy and then took the chain from around my neck.

Milo, it was such a relief to have that weight taken away. Even though she put another rope - a soft, light one - on me, I felt free. I knew I was safe and that she loved me, even though I'd never seen her before.

So I went with her. We walked out of that place, she helped me into the back of her big car and then we left. We left there forever. And I was happy.

I was a bit less happy when I got out of the car and there were lots and lots of excited dogs who wanted to say hello to me, but that lasted only a very short time. Then there was food and play and friends and love. I learned the words "Bravo" and was called "Silly Boy" and was able to grow strong and bounce and dance and wrestle. I knew then that my life was never going to be the same again.

And it wasn't. The Lovely Lady and the rest of Apollo's Angels saved me and brought me here and gave me everything I have. And for that I will love them all forever.

How clever are your people, Milo? I hate to say it, but sometimes mine are a little bit, well, dim. They do their best, but they don't always listen to what I'm telling them even though I make it as simple as possible for them.

For example, when they give me my breakfast and dinner, they have always put it in a bowl on the floor. Now, I don't need to tell you the obvious issues with that, but they just didn't seem to get it. I put up with it for a while but tried to let them know about the problem.

I whined a bit. I ate a bit. I gave a little woof. I ate another bit. I danced around a little. I ate another bit. They talked to me. I ate another bit. I really don't know how I could have made it any clearer, really.

Anyway, I think they must have talked to someone and had some help, because the other day they finally scattered my food on the floor without using a a bowl, so I can eat it properly. I still like to have them nearby in case I need something, but I think we've sorted out mealtimes for now anyway. They insist on keeping their own food up high though, which seems wrong to me.

Dad's holding my pyjamas now, so it's nearly time for bed, I think. I decided earlier to change my bed around, but Dad's put it back together again. Sometimes I think of all those other dogs out there who don't have comfy beds like ours, and that makes me very sad. They are all Good Dogs. Every single one of them.

Sleep well Milo. Maybe you'll hear my Angel in your dreams.

Your friend

Jackson

January 23rd 2022

Dear Milo

Hurrah! Mum's home!

She came home yesterday and I was so happy to see her. I gave her a good sniff all over to make sure everything was ok and then went into that full-body wag that I save for very special occasions. You know the one - when your tail wags so hard your bum starts to wobble and then your entire back half is jigging back and forth and then your front paws start to lift. And then how we danced!

Granny is well too, which also makes me glad. I like Granny very much and I know I'm her favourite grand-dog. She still has that cat however. I know because I could smell that it had been sleeping on Mum's stuff, which is a bit of a cheek. Yesterday I didn't care though, because Mum was home.

Dad was very pleased to have her home too. I looked after him very well, I think, but he's always better when Mum's about. The three of us danced for ages and ages and then they sat down in the food place and drank hot stuff. I just stood next to Mum and she rested her hand on my back and I was happy.

Yesterday was special for another reason too, mind you. I didn't realise it but according to Uncle Reefing yesterday was my birthday and now I'm four! Nobody knows when my real birthday is, so the Lovely Lady who rescued me decided that yesterday would be my day and wrote it down. Uncle Reefing has two birthdays. His official birthday is in the middle of the growing, and his real birthday is at the start of the hot. So there you go - my official birthday is at the end of the cold, just before the start of the growing. It was my friend Mala's birthday yesterday too. She was three and got a very smart scarf to wear. I didn't get a scarf, but I did get presents. A lot of them looked like the ones I got at Kiss-Miss mind you, but I got a hard proggly green thing to chew that tasted of veggies. Mum and Dad seemed very surprised that it disappeared quite as quickly as it did. I like birthdays. Good things happen on birthdays.

I was thinking about something while Mum was away and it was just Dad and me. Before I came here from the other place, when I lived with all those other dogs, we used to talk about where we came from and what had happened to us. I remember one dog - a big pointer boy like me, but younger - who had a very sad story. He went to live with his family when he was just a puppy and for a long time they were all very happy. Like all puppies he was small and cuddly and loved to play and to sleep.

And his family loved that and played with him and let him sleep when he needed it.

But then he grew, and he grew. He stopped sleeping so much, but still wanted to play all the time. And he wanted to run. And he wanted to hunt. And he wanted to meet girl dogs. Soon his family didn't want to play with him anymore and they didn't want to take him for walks, so he ended up like me - tied up outside, not able to run. But because he was still just a puppy he chewed things and he broke things and he pooed in the wrong place and he was too rough when they did want to play with him. He didn't know any better though. Nobody taught him the right way to do things or how to be a Good Dog.

Then he came to live with the Lovely Lady, and it all changed. She spent a long time helping him until it was time for him to go up in the air and go live with a new family who would love him and keep helping him learn until he knew he was a Good Boy.

I know now that sometimes it's not easy living with a dog like me. Some of us are big and some of us are little but we all need a lot of our people's time to let us run and hunt and sniff and just be pointers. On top of that, a lot of us need extra help because our lives up to now have been very hard. I know Dad didn't have much spare time while Mum was away, what with doing his work and looking after Uncle Reefing and looking after me.

I think what happened with the dog I met was that the people who took him as a puppy didn't love him but loved the IDEA of having a dog in their house. They thought it would be easy and when they got bored they could put him away for a while and get him out again when they wanted to. But of course you can't do that. So when they got tired of him they threw him away.

That's one of the reasons I love Mum and Dad. They know what I need and they give me the time and the space to be me and to be a real dog. I know that sometimes it's hard, and sometimes there are other things they would like to do but we're a family now and whatever they do will always include me.

And what will I do, Milo? I'll do the only things I can. I'll try to be a Good Boy and do the things that make them happy. I'll protect them. And I will give them all the love I have to give.

Goodnight Milo. Look after your Mum and Dad.

Your friend,

Jackson

January 30th 2022

Dear Milo

Hello! I hope you have been well and happy since I last wrote.

Mum and Dad have both been home all the time which was nice and we've had lots of walks and cuddles and play. It's still been cold, mind you, but the growing is coming really soon. I can feel it.

Are you brave, Milo? I bet you are. I'm not, I think. I'm very happy to go in the car or with loud bangs or the hoover or going into water and things like that but I get worried by a lot by things that don't really bother other dogs. I don't like the hot burny thing and still won't go into the room where it is. I don't like it when men carry sticks. And I'm scared of little dogs.

Something not nice happened the other day. There are some little dogs that live near here that we meet sometimes. They are always angry and shout at me and pull at their leads. This time though, their person dropped one of their leads and the little dog came running at me, yapping its head off. Dad tried to get between us but it kept coming and got behind me trying to bite my leg. I yelped and tried to run away but the little dog kept chasing and coming after me. Eventually the lady picked up the lead and they went away. I was very frightened and sad so put my tail between my legs and tried to make myself as small as I could. Dad didn't say anything but I knew he was really upset, but not with me. He got onto his knees in the middle of the field and gave me a big cuddle and I knew then it was going to be ok.

Most of the time dogs are angry or mean because they're scared or hurt or worried. But sometimes it's just who they are. Sometimes dogs just don't like people or other dogs and growl and bark and bite. I think the best thing to do is to not go near those dogs and not give them the chance to be mean. Some people can be like that too and only want to do and say things that hurt. The best thing to do with those people is just stay away from them and ignore them if you can.

I'm trying to be braver though. Uncle Reefing says you can't be brave unless you're scared first. He says real bravery is doing something even though you are scared. Doing something BECAUSE you are scared.

I think I was brave tonight. The burny thing was on and even though it's quite near where I sleep I didn't whine and I didn't bark but instead got onto my bed and snuggled down. Mum came later and gave me cuddles and put my blankie on me so I think I was a Good Boy.

Maybe someday the burny thing won't bother me at all. I think I'd like that.

I met Lola when we went to see Uncle Reefing at The Yard today and she told me she made a new friend. His name is Buddy and he's a very little Black Labrador puppy. I'm four now, so it's a long time since I was a puppy but there are some things I remember. I remember how warm and safe my mummy was and how she looked after me when I was very tiny. I remember how big my paws were and how sometimes I would trip over myself when I tried to run. And I remember when I had to go and live with The Man. Dogs learn about life when they are little. Most are lucky and get to live with families who love them but dogs like me don't get that chance when we're puppies. Instead we need to find special people who will help us learn even though we're older and bigger and not as cute and innocent and cuddly. It would have been nice if I had found Mum and Dad when I was a puppy.

I think I wouldn't be so scared if I had known them when I was little and had grown up knowing how much they loved me. Thanks to the Lovely Lady and Apollo's Angels I'm here with my family now though, and that's enough for me.

I've been a Very Good Boy on our walks since I last wrote. Most of the time, when we're in the fields and I'm on my long lead, Dad doesn't hold onto it at all.

Sometimes I even have to carry it myself! I sit very patiently when it's time to put leads on or take them off and I wait until Dad tells me I can go before I run off. I still don't always hear him when he calls but I'm getting better. I found him a lovely pheasant in Uncle Reefing's field today and was very proud of myself when I made it fly.

It's time to sleep now so I'm going to say goodnight. Be good, Milo, and stay away from the bad people.

Your friend

Jackson

Oh deer – Eau de fox – An only dog

February 6th 2022

Dear Milo

I hope you are well and happy.

I am very well thank you and having a wonderful time. Dad and I had such an exciting walk today I'm still a bit bouncy just remembering it.

We went to The Yard like we usually do and Dad brought Uncle Reefing into his house and put his pyjamas on and then he attached the really long lead to my clippy strappy thing and off we went into Uncle Reefing's field. Sometimes I find pheasants in there so I really like Uncle Reefing's field. This time though I smelled something different. I ran back and forth to find where it was but that wasn't hard. The scent, Milo! It was big and red and brown and gold and filled my entire head so I followed it and then suddenly, right in front of me, was this huge big deer! To be honest, he wasn't actually that big, really. He was only a little bit bigger than me, but he could jump! He jumped out of the bushes and bounced away through the long grass. I wanted to chase him but could only go as far as the long lead let me, and Dad wasn't going anywhere. I leaned on the end and whined and barked until I realised Dad was calling my name so I went back to him instead.

I was still really excited though and bounced around Dad for a bit, telling him what had happened. I was so excited I didn't even want the yummy he was offering me. Dad made me wait for a while, which I couldn't understand as it meant the deer got away. Then I realised that I could search for him all over again!

So I did. I ran back and forth until I thought I smelled something and then I sniffed a bit more and then a bit more until I was sure. And then I followed. I followed exactly where the deer had been all the way around the big field, past the houses and the place where the children play and then when we got to the big prickly bush, I stopped. Then I crept up veeerrry sloowwly and did my best point.

As Dad came up behind me (he was very slow, and I'm not sure he was as interested as I was in finding the deer) the deer burst out of the bush and lots of little birds flew out and it was amazing. It was like Kiss-Miss. I wanted to follow again but I think Dad's arms were tired because he made us go back to Uncle Reefing's house instead. I was so excited I kept bouncing around and looking for the deer again and then bouncing again. It was brilliant!

I've been so good since I last wrote you wouldn't believe it. I spend longer and longer every day without any lead at all and I always come back when I hear my name. As you know, I take Mum or Dad for a long walk in the middle of the day, just to get them out and away from the people-box. Once we get to the track, my long lead goes on, but usually nobody holds it now and it just sits on the ground. Then we go up along beside the ditch (and sometimes into it) and I get to look for birds and get yummies when I come back when my name is called and I get to run around and it's great fun.

After another while the long lead is usually taken off and then I can run around without it trailing after me. The best bit though - the really really exciting bit - is when the ball comes out! I love my ball. It was a present from my friends Pepper and Copper and it's my favourite thing in the world. I think that sometimes I like it even more than I like looking for birds. Anyway, Mum or Dad throw the ball (Dad is better because he can throw it further) and I chase after it as fast as I can and pick it up. Sometimes I get so excited I drop it and it bounces off again which means I get to chase it twice! When I catch it, I run back as fast as I can and drop it so they can throw it again. Usually I get a yummy too, but I have to Sit for that to happen. When we get closer to home I have to Sit and Wait while they fuss about with my lead again and then we go home.

I love going out without my lead. I get to run ever so much. I think I'm very fit now and can run faster than ever. It's funny to think that not so long ago, I didn't think this would ever happen and I'd always have to be on my lead. The invisible rope between me and Mum and Dad is so strong now, I don't think anything could ever break it.

We have lots of little birds come into our garden because there's lots of food for them. Sometimes there's bread and if I get the chance I take it and hide it in my bed for later. Mum and Dad don't like that though and take it away which is really unfair. I keep watching the little birds through the door though, just in case.

The nice lady who gave me Swan came to visit yesterday. I brought Swan to show her and sat next to her while she and Mum drank hot stuff. Mum thought Swan was a bit grubby so he and Monkey and Phezzie and Raccoon spent most of today in the hot swirly thing and then in the hot clanky thing. When he came out he was very bright and smelled of flowers and he was hot! He's in my bed now though.

It's getting a bit late so I think I'll go check and make sure he's OK. Sleep well Milo. Be a Good Boy and always go back when you're called.

Your very good friend,

Jackson

February 14th 2022

Dear Milo

What a yucky day it's been! So wet and windy that I've had to have my coat on for the first time in ages. The nice thing about it is being able to come back to my lovely warm and dry home where I get rubbed all over with a fluffy towel and it's like getting great big cuddles and playing a game at the same time. The only thing that bothers me is that the hot burny thing has come back and the people insist on sitting near it. I stay outside the room and look in every now and then to make sure they're still OK. I don't cry like I used to, but I think I'll never like that burny thing.

Mum had to go stay with Granny again but everyone is fine and she's back home now. Dad and I don't like it when she's away, but it's wonderful when she comes back. It takes me a little while to make sure it's her, but when I am sure I get very excited and spin around and around and wag my tail so very much. I hope my being shy at first doesn't upset her, because I love her very much, but sometimes she smells a bit different and I don't need to tell you how much I trust my nose!

I'm still being a Good Boy when we go for walks. Dad hardly ever holds my long lead now and there's no lead at all for longer and longer every day. Dad does this funny thing sometimes. Usually when he calls my name I run over to him to see what he wants and then I get something nice to eat. If I don't go to him though, he says my name again and then he turns around and runs away! Of course, I'm not going to be left behind so I immediately run straight after him as fast as I can. Then he stops and turns around and I get cuddles and yummies and told I'm a Good Boy. Mum hasn't been on a long walk with us for a little while, so she was really proud of me when she saw how good I am.

I can really feel The Growing now. It's in the air and in the ground and in everything. The grass is starting to get longer and thicker and there are more smells to sniff and the little white flowery things are back again. When Dad gets back from The Yard these days he's usually covered in Uncle Reefing fur. Uncle Reefing says he's really itchy and needs lots of brushing to keep his coat nice and clean and shiny, although he's very hairy right now. Do you like being brushed, Milo? Uncle Reefing loves it but I'm not so sure. I try to be good but it's tickly and then it turns into a game where I take the brush and run around while Mum and Dad try to get it back. It's great fun but I think I probably enjoy it a little bit more than they do.

I was back at the V.E.T again to have more needles stuck in me, just like what happened in the other place, shortly before I came here. I didn't like it, although the man was very nice and gentle but Uncle Reefing says it's to stop me from getting sick. He has needles too for the same reason, and so do Mum and Dad, even. Do you have needles, Milo? Apparently, as well as stopping you from getting sick, it stops other dogs around you from getting sick too. Maybe if we all have needles, nobody will get sick at all. Wouldn't that be great.

Something else happened while we were walking the other day. I was off the lead as usual and we met the big tall man who lives nearby. He and Dad stopped to talk so I waited very patiently next to them until they were finished and Dad and I walked on. Then I smelled it. It was heavenly - rich and dark and heavy and irresistible - and it was really, really close. I looked at Dad and as soon as he looked away, I grabbed my chance and went for it. Dad can be surprisingly quick when he wants, so I had barely got my ear into it before he grabbed my clippy strappy thing and dragged me away from it. I'm sending you a picture of my ear.

When we got home Dad used a lot of his special words while I wriggled about as he tried to wash that lovely smell off me. It took ages and I was very sad. My Whippet neighbour Izzy managed to cover her entire side and had to have an actual bath in the middle of the day. She says it was absolutely worth it and nothing quite compares to Eau de Fox.

And I'm going to leave it there, Milo. Be brave with your needles and enjoy The Growing.

Your friend

Jackson

February 27th 2022

Dear Milo

I hope you are well and enjoyed the sunshine today. Wasn't it lovely? Raccoon was so happy he dug a hole in the grassy bit. I got blamed as usual.

The Growing is definitely here now. The flowery things are out and the grass is higher and the days are getting nice and long. And the smells, of course! There are more birds around and there are amazing smells everywhere. There are so many smells that it's getting harder to hear Dad when he calls me so I have been spending a little more time on the long lead than I like. Uncle Reefing says I've gone backwards a little bit, but not to worry about it. He says that when we learn new things, it can push some things we already know out of our heads so we forget and then have to learn it again. It happens to everyone, he says, and won't take long for me to get it all back and be a Good Boy again. I really hope so. I love being able to run and play without the lead, and I don't want Dad to be disappointed with me.

Uncle Reefing's field is particularly exciting right now. It's huge with long grass and trees and bushes and thorny stuff around the edges. Milo, you wouldn't believe that number of birds and mousies and spiders and bunnies and hares that live there. Last time, I found a partridge and made him fly and Dad thought that was great. Then I found a hare and made him run. Dad was less happy about that, I think. He held onto my long lead and wouldn't let me go any further, even though I jumped around and whined and barked. By the time he let me go the hare was long gone and we had to go home so I had no chance of finding him again which made me a bit sad.

Do you ever wonder what it would be like to have a brother or sister, Milo? I do, sometimes. Often I think it would be lovely to have company and someone to play with all the time and to sleep on and to be my friend. Other times I worry about it, because you never know, when you get a new brother or sister, if you're going to be friends or not, even if you're from the same litter. We're all different and sometimes that doesn't work very well. I worry about Mum and Dad too. They work very hard to look after me and after each other, and I think that another dog would leave them very little time to do anything else.

There's one other thing that worries me, though, and I'm afraid it might be very selfish. I'm scared that if another dog were to join our family it would spoil what we have. Maybe Mum and Dad wouldn't be able to spend so much time with me. Maybe our walks wouldn't be as much fun. Maybe the new dog would be so nice that Mum and Dad would prefer them to me?

I think that it's best for now that I'm an only dog. I'm still learning how to be a Good Dog but maybe someday we'll be ready to welcome someone else and I'll be able to help them like Uncle Reefing helps me.

I heard about some amazing people that I must tell you about. As you know, there are lots and lots of dogs like me in the place I came from. Well, some people, even though they can't give a forever home, welcome them into their families over here and look after them and help them learn until they find a family of their own. Isn't that wonderful? It's called "Fostering". These are very special people and we're lucky to have them. Of course, sometimes it doesn't go exactly to plan and they finally work out that the dog's forever home is right there with them, but that's another happy story.

I saw someone the other day I haven't seen for ages - Bertie the Boxer! We didn't exactly bounce around when we met each other, but it was nice to see him in any case. We've had our differences, but he's still my neighbour and my friend so I'll treat him with respect and play when he asks and leave him alone when he asks, and he does the same for me. It's just the neighbourly thing to do. And his mum gives me sausage when we meet, so that's always good too.

It's bedtime again so goodnight Milo. Look after your friends and neighbours.

Your friend

Jackson

Dad takes a tumble – My friend Flicka – Gotcha Day – Home thoughts

March 6th 2022

Dear Milo

I hope you are well. I am very well thank you.

We've had a quiet time since I last wrote, just enjoying my home and spending lots of time with Mum and Dad. Mum has been up in the air again, but Dad and I managed while she was away. I much prefer it when she's home though, and so does Dad. It's just better when we're together.

Did I tell you about my ball? It was a present from my friends Pepper and Copper and is probably my favourite thing in the whole world. We bring it on walks and my favourite is when we're on our way home and Dad takes it out of his bag and throws it for me and I mostly bring it back for him to throw again.

Well one day we were playing near the deep muddy wet bit when I got a bit distracted by a bird and accidentally dropped it. And it rolled. And rolled.

And rolledreallyfastintothewater. We could see it under some bushes, bobbing up and down so when Dad told me to go get it I went straight in. Down, down into the water which came right up to my tummy. I could see the ball and pushed my way as far as I could but whenever I went to pick it up it bobbed just out of reach. I tried and tried but just couldn't get it and got very frustrated, barking and yelping at it. In the end Dad called me back up and gave me a cuddle and told me it was ok, but I was very sad to lose my ball.

The next day however, Dad brought a big stick when we went out and when we got to where the ball was he climbed down into the mud and used the stick to get it back! Dad is very clever. Then after all that he threw it for me and it bounced off a rock, flew into the field and we lost it for a second time. I was very upset all over again.

When I first got here I didn't like new people all that much and would always stay away from people I didn't know. I realised just yesterday that I'm very different now. We had a visitor come to the house - someone I've met a couple of times before - and I went straight to the door to welcome her, wagging my tail all the time where in the past I'd have waited a little bit and stuck beside Mum or Dad or hidden in the room where Dad works. Then I realised I've been doing this for most people - the nice man who brings the food to our door, people we meet on our walks, the man that wipes the windows - everyone! Rosie and Uncle Reefing are very proud of me. Uncle Reefing says that if you are nice to people, they'll be nice to you. Apparently when he was young he wasn't nice to people until he met Dad, and Dad helped him learn. I think Mum and Dad have helped me learn too and I'm very glad they did.

I learned another lesson too. If something is important to you, you must never give up. Never. Keep trying. Keep looking. Keep hoping. No matter what you are up against, when you have your people and your friends with you, you can make good things happen. I told Rosie about my ball being lost so she and I and her people and my people went to look for it and some other people we met helped us too. And you know what?

We found it.

We worked together and helped each other and we found it. So that was what I learned. Like Apollo, you should never give up. Even when you think what you love is lost, there is always hope. When you have friends and people to help you, you can always have hope.

Goodnight Milo. Sleep well and have peaceful dreams.

Your good friend

Jackson

March 13th 2022

Dear Milo

What a lovely time I've had since I last wrote! Mum didn't spend any time at all on her people-box, and I got to stay with her all the time, apart from when I was sleepy and put myself on my bed. We played in the grassy place and went for so many walks.

One walk was a bit odd, mind you. Instead of her normal coat, Mum put on a really bright top and we went outside to find lots and lots of other people in bright tops carrying bags and long grabby sticks, which was very strange.

You know how, when you're on your walk, you get told off if you start sniffing around the messy horrible people-stuff that's on the ground and in the hedges? Well, this time all the people were actually looking for it. Then they'd pick it up with the grabby stick, screw up their face, and shove it into the big bag they were carrying. We went all around the place where we live and found lots and lots of little bits of papery stuff and bags and glass things. I found something that used to be a mousey but had turned into food and had a quick snack to keep me going, but apparently that makes me A Disgrace and Mum had her disappointed face on.

There were lots of people and lots of dogs there but (apart from the mousey bit) I was on my best behaviour and made lots of new friends. Everyone was very good and worked hard and it all looked very neat and tidy afterwards. I don't know why people throw things away like that. Maybe it's like picking up poo. Everyone should do it but there are a small few who don't and spoil it for everyone else. I don't see how it can be hard to bring your stuff home with you - Mum and Dad do it all the time.

I'm meeting lots of new people these days. When they come to our house I sometimes try to be fierce but I'm not very good at it, I'm afraid. I can make my front end do it and I have a really good big woof, but my back end always lets me down. Last night we had visitors come to eat food and while I had a good bark when they arrived, I couldn't stop wagging my tail all the time so they weren't scared at all. In fact, when I woofed they paid no attention to me at all, but I got cuddles when I stopped. I need to have a think about that.

We went back to the place with the glass doors and all the planty things too. We walked around inside the huge big house and I was sticking close to Dad when this lady on wheels stopped to talk. She looked very strange and I wasn't sure at all, but Mum and Dad weren't worried so I gave her a sniff and she patted me gently. That seemed to make her happy so I was happy too. I like that place but didn't get to bring a toy home this time. Probably for the best. We don't want to risk another Monkey.

Something else lovely happened too. You know how my favourite ball went missing and we found it again? It seems that my friends Pepper and Copper heard about it and sent me more new balls in case it happens again! The nice man that brings me biscuits and gives papery things to my people brought a box that had my name on and they were inside. I promise I will take very, very good care of them.

It was such a lovely surprise and I'm very lucky to have such good friends.

And I'm lucky to have you for my friend too.

Goodnight Milo. Maybe you'll find some mousies in your dreams.

Your good friend

Jackson

March 20th 2022

Dear Milo

Today reminded me a little bit of the other place, it was so lovely and warm. I even got to do a little bit of sunbathing outside our house, which was nice, while Dad pushed the noisy thing up and down the grass. It's funny, but I hardly ever think about the other place now. It's almost like this has always been my home and Mum and Dad and Uncle Reefing have always been my family. Just thinking about that makes me happy.

Dad and Uncle Reefing were very not happy the other day. According to Uncle Reefing, they were trotting along in the big field when a dog popped out of the long grass right in front of them. Uncle Reefing got a terrible fright and jumped around and because Dad wasn't paying attention he fell off Uncle Reefing's back! It was a long way down and Dad is very old but he wasn't hurt. Uncle Reefing accidentally broke some of the strappy things he wears though, which made him sad.

They weren't upset with the dog, who was only doing doggy things, but they were both definitely upset with the dog's person, who wasn't keeping an eye out and making sure they weren't going somewhere they weren't supposed to be. Dogs can't read and don't know that sort of thing so it's up to their people to look out for them and guide them. This dog's person didn't, and apparently they scuttled off without even checking that Dad and Uncle Reefing were OK. That's a bad thing and we would never do that, because Mum and Dad would always make sure that I'm safe and so are the people we might meet. Some people need to be trained properly I think.

Do you remember the place I went ages ago where Dad left me and I cried until he came back? Well, we went there again. I've been there a few times now and do you know, I think it's just not for me. I don't know if I was unhappy because Dad was unhappy or he was unhappy because I was unhappy, but we're not going back there again. Sometimes, when you're a special dog like I am, you need to be looked after differently and sometimes people aren't able to see that. And that's OK. To look after special dogs you need special people.

I made another new friend! One day Dad and I got in the car and went to The Yard. Instead of going into Uncle Reefing's field though, we walked a different way and went to a house I hadn't been to before. A nice lady opened the door and then I met Flicka. Flicka is a very pretty little Cocker Spaniel and she lives near Uncle Reefing. She's only one, so still just a puppy but when Mum and Dad have to be somewhere else I'm going to come to her house and stay with her. I'm a little bit nervous about it but she's very nice and her Mum is kind so I'm sure it will be OK. Flicka says her Mum knows all about hunting dogs so we'll get on just fine.

We've found a new place to play near home, too. It's a big field with a high fence to stop stuff getting in and it has lots of toys and places to climb and sniff and pee on. There aren't many pee-mails there yet, but the ones I've sniffed have been very interesting. Best of all, because of the high fence, I can run around without any lead on at all. When you come to visit I'll show it to you. Rosie and I are going to go back there very soon. Mum and Dad like it too because while I'm running around having a great time they can sit in the little house and not worry about anything.

Do you like flowery things, Milo? There are lots of them here and I saw some big bright noddy ones today. They seem very happy and people always seem to smile when they see them too. I'm starting to really like flowery things. Maybe I should help Mum take care of ours. I think she'd like that.

I love these days, when Mum and Dad and Uncle Reefing and I spend lots of time together and I can snooze in the sunshine and my tummy is full and I can play with my friends. I'm happy Milo. I'm really, really happy.

Goodnight Milo. I hope you're as happy as I am.

Your friend

Jackson

March 27ᵗʰ 2022

Dear Milo

I had such an amazing day earlier this week – it was like Kiss-Miss and my birthday and all kinds of good things rolled into one. I got cuddles and yummies and got a new Phezzie and was allowed to do whatever I wanted all day. Dad put a coloury cloth thing around my neck. I have no idea what it was, but it looked very smart.

Uncle Reefing told me why the day was so special. Apparently it was my Gotcha Day which means all the seasons have passed since I came to live here - the growing, the hot, the brown and the cold - and now they're going to go around again. That's a very long time. It's so long that sometimes I forget where I came from and what my life before was like.

In the other place, I didn't have a real home, I was always hungry and it was usually too hot or too cold. I lived outside and had a chain around my neck all the time and was scared of The Man. I did my best but I was still hit and shouted at and was very, very lonely.

How things have changed since that night I went up in the air with all those other dogs and came here to meet Mum and Dad in that very strange place with all the cars. I was so scared, Milo. So scared. But I think Mum and Dad knew me and loved me before that night, even. And now I love them too.

I've learned so much since then and am still learning and doing new things every day.

I've learned how to live in a house, and to ask to go outside when I need a wee or a poo. I get lots and lots of food and now eat up everything without any fuss at all. My bed is warm and cosy and I'm really good at going to lie on it when I'm asked to. That's where I stay all night when Mum and Dad are sleeping, even if I'm awake and guarding our house.

When I hear the word "Sit" I plop my bottom on the ground and wait until I'm told I'm a Good Boy and when I hear "Down" I lie down flat and stay there. When I hear "Off" it means that I have to give over what I'm holding in my mouth or I have to stop trying to climb up on Dad. I've learned that when Mum and Dad are talking on the people-box, I get put on my bed if I use my teeth to nibble on their elbow, but if I put my paw on them they'll stop and talk to me.

When we're out, I know that when they call my name and say "Come" I should run to them as fast as I can and I'll get yummy stuff and lots of cuddles. That one's still really hard because of all the birds, but we're still working on it. I'm a really big boy now and you can't see my bones through my skin anymore, but I can run so fast you wouldn't believe it. I'm even faster than Rosie.

Rosie. I have so many friends now. You and Rosie and Lola and Bertie and Pepper and Copper and Amber and Wellie and Scrumpy and Bonnie and Flicka and Ivy and Ted and Scooby and Meera and so many more. We get to sniff and play bitey-face and wrestle and run around and do all the lovely things I wasn't able to do in the other place.

I know what toys are now too. I'd never seen one before I came here but I have loads now! HedgePig and Hare are the oldest and most special, but I love that the people keep giving me presents and every single toy is wonderful.

And then there are all the people - the Lovely Lady who first saved me and all the other Apollo's Angels who helped me even though I've never met them. I see now that most people are good and kind. I think was unlucky that I had to live with The Man and most people in the other place are good too. The people I meet now are very nice. We talk to them when we see them on our walks and I welcome them when they come to our house, although I always make sure that my family is safe first, mind you.

My family. My family and my home. Mum and Dad and Uncle Reefing are the most important things in my life. More important than me, even. I didn't really understand what family meant before, but I do now. Family will love you and take care of you and help you, even when you make mistakes. They will open the door when you want to come in and they will cuddle you and tell you you're a Good Boy even when you think you're not. They will never hurt you and they will always, always come back for you. And I'll do all those things for them too. Apart from the door, of course, but I'd do that too if I was able.

So that's it, Milo. That's my life now, and it is shiny and happy and lovely. It feels just like when I was a tiny puppy. I'm warm and comfy and when my tummy is full and I'm feeling sleepy I can snuggle up to Mum and Dad and they'll stroke my ears and tell me how good and clever and handsome I am. And then I'll fall asleep, knowing that I will always be safe and always be loved.

Forever.

Here in my forever home.

Goodnight Milo. Thank you for listening and for being my friend. Be a Good Dog and keep looking after your people and your home.

Your good friend

Jackson

*Time with Flicka - An update on The Foot –
Uncle Reefing's thoughts on dressage*

June 5th 2022

Dear Milo

I hope you are well. I am very well thank you.

It's been a while since I last wrote and we've had a very busy time recently so I thought I'd give you an update on what we're doing.

I think I told you about my new friend Flicka who I stay with sometimes? Now, if Mum has to go up in the air and Dad has to go to the big glass house, then I spend the day with Flicka and her Mum who live very near Uncle Reefing. I was a bit unsure at first but now I love it and almost drag Dad through the door when we get there early in the morning. Flicka and I have a great time playing and snoozing and going for really long walks. Her Mum smells like flowers and there are little people there too. I like the little people but they're sometimes a little bit unsteady so I help them by letting them lean on me. Lots of my other friends stay there too since I started so there's usually someone else for Flicka and me to play with which is nice.

The grass is growing really high here now. Is it the same where you are? Sometimes I find it hard to see Mum and Dad so have to bounce around a bit until I spot them. I'm being very good on my walks and am allowed off the lead again. I think that there are so many dogs with long hair living here that find it hard to walk in the long grass, the track has nearly disappeared! Luckily with my short hair I don't find it so hard, but Mum and Dad are very careful to look in my ears and in my paws when we get home to make sure nothing from the grass gets stuck in there because that can cause a lot of trouble, you know.

Milo, I finally got to go to The Foot yesterday! I think I didn't hear Rosie properly when she was telling me about it because it's actually called The Feet. Everything else was exactly as she described though. Dad gave me a really good brush, put on the smart collar I got at Kiss-Miss and off we went to the big green bit in the middle of the place where we all live. It was amazing! A little bit too amazing at first, if I'm honest and I was a little bit scared because of all the people and all the noise but Dad looked after me and I looked after him and we were fine.

There were little white flappy houses with all kinds of stuff in them but Mum wouldn't let Dad get anything which made him sad. He was allowed to get a big glass of scummy brown water though, and that made him happy again. He also bought this incredible thing called a

240

hamburger. Milo, I've never smelled anything like it. It didn't smell like ham, but it was big and warm and juicy and made me dribble. Now, I don't usually bother too much with food but this was a different thing altogether. I sat on the ground and couldn't take my eyes off it. Dad gave me a little bit and it was wonderful with soft bread and juicy meat and creamy cheese and I really, really, really want to try it again very soon.

Lots of people stopped to talk to Mum and Dad at The Feet. They all wanted to talk about me for some reason. It happens all the time when we go out so I'm quite used to it now. I don't think people see many pointers in this place so they want to learn all about me and where I came from.

There were a lot of little people there too and they all wanted to talk to me as well. They were very good though - first they'd ask my Mum and Dad if it was allowed, and then they'd let me have a sniff and then if I thought it was OK I'd let them stroke my head or my ears. I liked these little ones very much. I think they must have very good Mums and Dads to tell them the proper way to get to know a dog.

Then, near the end of the day, we had the people show. It was very exciting. We had to lead our people around this little grassy place and then a lady would come and talk to us and at the end she gave a ribbon to the dog whose person she liked best. We didn't win that one, but

Rosie did and we were very happy for her. Then there was another one where we had to walk our people around while a jingly noise played and when the noise stopped our people had to ask us to sit down. The last one to sit down had to go out and then we started again. I was really good at this. As soon as Dad's hand went up I plopped my bum on the ground.

We didn't win, sadly, even though I think we did better than some of the others. I didn't mind, but I think Dad would have liked a ribbon and was a bit upset. I'll win one for him next year.

I was telling Uncle Reefing about it all later and he said it was like bucking dressage (I think he said bucking, but he was eating at the time). He says at least with shoe-jumping it's either up or down and you don't have some (another word I didn't know) in a hat deciding if you're in or out. I didn't understand very much of what he was talking about but he REALLY doesn't like dressage, whatever that is.

He did say something I found very easy to understand though. He says we're all winners, him and me and Mum and Dad. We found each other. With all the horses and dogs and people in the world, we found each other and there's no bigger or better prize than that.

Goodnight Milo. Keep the grass out of your ears.

Your good friend

Jackson

Author's Note

In case you hadn't already realised, Jackson's letters are based on his real life and his actual experiences. The thing about real life, though, is that you can't control it. If this was just a story, this next piece wouldn't have happened.

One Sunday evening at the end of October Jackson was a little off-colour so we took him to the vet the next day, where a precautionary blood test showed he was in acute renal failure, from an unknown cause. Intensive treatment started immediately both at our vet and at the internal medicine specialist to whom he was transferred but sadly they couldn't save him.

Jackson died peacefully at midday on Monday October 24th 2022. As usual, he was happy and excited to see us, but got tired very quickly. We knelt down and he climbed into my lap as he always did, then drifted off with a big sigh, getting strokes and cuddles and kisses from me and from his Mum. He was comfortable and content, showing us that he loved us, and acknowledging our love in return.

Subsequent tests showed that despite testing negative the previous year and showing no outward symptoms whatsoever, Jackson had developed leishmaniasis which ultimately took him from us.

To me, Jackson was far more than a pet or a companion animal. He was a link to my lovely father who passed away in 2020 - it made my heart soar when I first realised that Jackson looked at me the same way Granddad Pollock looked at my dad. He was a link to the happiest of my childhood memories. He made me write, for the first time in decades. Jackson was innocence. He was good. He was joy and happiness and gentleness and trust. Above all he was total and unconditional love. Like most rescues, he had every right to hate and fear people, but he didn't. Instead he launched himself wholeheartedly into our family and into our lives. Jackson's was the purest soul I have ever met.

Jackson was with us for just 18 months and it seems terribly, terribly unfair that he was taken from us so quickly. We try to console ourselves however that during the short time he spent with us he was safe, happy and loved. I like to think he packed all his living into that time and forgot completely about his old life in Cyprus. I am so incredibly grateful to the team at Apollo's Angels for bringing him into our lives and giving us the chance to be part of his.

Writing the letter that follows was one of the most difficult things I've ever done, but I owed it to him to finish his story and share the ultimate reality of having a dog in your life.

Thank you for sharing it with me.

Diarmuid Fahy

October 24th 2022

Dear Milo

This my last letter, I'm afraid, as I think I'm going to have a huge new adventure soon.

I've been feeling quite poorly for a little while, you see, and I think the time is coming for me to go away. I'm not frightened of going away. We all have to go away sometime, although I think it would have been nice to stay just a little bit longer. It's a bit of a bugger, as Uncle Reefing would say. I'm not sure what's going to happen but I think I'm going to see Grandad Pollock and Dad's Mum and Dad, and Apollo, and Gracie and we'll be able to run and play and have a wonderful time together and not worry about anything or be scared or have any pain whatsoever.

Mum and Dad will be sad, I think, but not for too long I hope. I know they will never ever forget me, but I still want them to be happy. I have had such a lovely time and so many adventures, and I want them to remember all the good bits and not just the sad part at the end. I know Uncle Reefing and Rosie will look after them, and maybe in time they'll be ready to make room in their hearts for someone else alongside me.

It started last week, when my tummy hurt a little and I felt a bit ill and didn't want my food, so Mum and Dad took me to see the V.E.T. They helped me feel a better for a little while, and stole a little bit of my blood again. I was very good and wasn't scared and sat very quietly for Dad while they did it, and then we went home. A short while later though, we were in the car again and went right back to the vet's house. There, the nice people helped me feel better straight away, but I had to stay with them for a while. Mum and Dad weren't there but I knew the nice people were trying to help me so I did everything they asked. I still felt quite poorly though, so a while later Mum and Dad came back and we went in the car to another vet house a long way away. It was nighttime when we got there but the place was big and bright and very smart. There I met another very nice lady who, after talking for ages to Mum and Dad, took my lead and we went to a place where there was a lovely soft bed. I went to sleep straight away as I was very tired.

The next few days are a bit confused, I'm afraid. The nice people helped take my pain away, and sat with me when I was eating and gave me lots of cuddles and told me what a good and handsome boy I was. I missed Mum and Dad terribly, but they came to see me every single day and I was always so happy to see them. Even if I felt poorly, I still wagged my tail as hard as I could and showed them I loved them, and they did the same to me.

I know I'm not getting better though. The nice people are doing their best to help me but it's just my time. Today has been wonderful. The lady came to see me this morning and took away most of my pain and even though I wasn't hungry I ate a little bit of food because I knew it would make her happy. Then we went for a little walk in the sunshine and I got to stop and sniff as much as I wanted until we came to a door and when we went inside Mum and Dad were there! I wagged and wagged my tail and even gave a little bounce, I was so happy to see them. That made me a bit tired though, so I sat down on the big fluffy bed they had put there for me. Mum and Dad got down on the floor with me then, so I lay down and put my paws and my head in their laps.

And that's where I am now, snuggled up with my family, warm and happy and safe. They're cuddling me and stroking my ears and kissing my head and all the pain is gone. I don't know if I've ever been happier, Milo. I can feel their love for me, and I love them so much it feels like I'll burst. Mum is talking to me and her voice is high and bright and clear. She lifts my heart and simply hearing her just gives me so much joy. Dad's voice is softer and deeper and I can feel it rumble through me as he presses his face to mine. He's calling me his Beautiful Boy and saying "Bravo, big lad", just like he did the very first time we saw each other. I feel so safe and I know that we will always be with each other in our hearts, no matter how far apart we are. This is where I'm supposed to be. These are my people. This is my family. This is home.

I'm feeling very sleepy now, Milo, so I think I'll have a little snooze. I'll just close my eyes for a little bit and then we'll see what happens next. I know it's going to be lovely.

Goodbye Milo. Be good. I'll see you in your dreams.

Your friend

Jackson

About the author

Diarmuid Fahy was born and raised in the hills of County Clare in the west of Ireland, surrounded by fields and forests and lakes. After a time in university where academic distinction was inversely proportional to the amount of fun he had, he embarked on an equestrian career in the world of showjumping. Tragically, this was cut short by a lack of talent combined with the development of some expensive habits such as eating and living in a house, so he eventually drifted back into the real world, all the better for the experience. He now works in the space sector, which people who know him feel to be quite appropriate.

Diarmuid currently lives in Oxfordshire with the oh-so-patient Julia, his horse Reefing and their Cyprus rescue GSP Castor.

"My Name is Jackson" is his first book.

Acknowledgements

This book would never have existed were it not for Apollo's Angels/Rehoming Cyprus Pointers and the incredible things they do both in Cyprus and in the UK. My thanks go to Lena Ashton, Janice McNaughton, Donna Kyriacou and Susan Hall for their tireless work in the most difficult of circumstances, and for gifting us the opportunity to have Jackson in our lives.

Jackson made friends all over the world, but some of his closest were right here with us, so my thanks go to Milo, Lorna and Tim Sellick, and Rosie, Alison and Tom Harrison. The love and support you showed us in good times and bad means the world.

To Teresa, Mary and Mario Purtill, who encouraged me to write and who helped keep me on the straight and narrow as only family can.

To my wonderful old friends Peadar O'Guilin and Triona Marren-O'Grady who (alongside Lorna Sellick and Mary Purtill) helped me with the nuts and bolts of putting this book together.

To Kathy Tiernan, who created the beautiful illustrations – you captured Jackson perfectly.

There are too many people to mention individually, but special thanks go to Dawn Fleming-Burt, Hilary Mudge, Katie Robinson, Lucy Willetts, Maria Robertson, Maurice, Pepper and Copper Hawkins, Nicola Thain, Sharon Hewen, Sue Hebb, Sue Rose, Tracy Payne and many, many others. Becoming an internet personality was not something that was ever planned for Jackson, but the online friends we made were a source of great joy to us, and the support and genuine depth of feeling that people showed when Jackson left us was one of the bright lights in a terrible time.

And to all Jackson's doggy friends: Milo, Rosie, Lola, Bertie, Welly, Bonnie, Scrumpy, Ivy, Pepper, Copper, Flicka, Cleo, Ted, Scooby, Meera, Wilbur and all the others. Thank you for all being Good Dogs. You remind us every day of the people we can be.

Made in United States
Troutdale, OR
11/11/2023